English Skills

Published by Collins
An imprint of HarperCollins*Publishers*
The News Building
1 London Bridge Street
London
SE1 9GF

Browse the complete Collins catalogue at
www.collinseducation.com

© HarperCollins*Publishers* Limited 2011, on behalf of the author

First published in 2006 by Folens Limited.

ISBN-13: 978-0-00-743723-8

British Library Cataloguing in Publication Data
A catalogue record for this publication is available from the British Library.

Every effort has been made to trace copyright holders and to obtain their permission for the use of copyright material. The authors and publishers will gladly receive any information enabling them to rectify any error or omission in subsequent editions.

Editor: Geraldine Sowerby
Layout artist: Patricia Hollingsworth
Illustrations: Tony Randell
Cover design: Martin Cross
Editorial consultant: Helen Whittaker

Printed and bound by CPI Group (UK) Ltd, Croydon, CR0 4YY

Contents

Reading

A   **Read the story.**

Rescue

The dog at once jumped off the bank and in a few seconds reached the child and caught it firmly. Then he turned to swim back, but the swift-flowing water had got hold of him. Bravely he struggled and lifted the child out of the water but his powerful efforts to stem the current were in vain. Each moment he was carried still further down until he was on the brink of the fall, which, though not high, was the most dangerous on the river. He raised himself high out of the stream with the *vigour* of his last struggle and then fell over into the *abyss*.

By this time the poor mother, as if she had *anticipated* the result, was already in a canoe, as close to the fall as it was possible for her to go with safety. The canoe danced like a cockle-shell on the turmoil of waters as the mother stood with uplifted paddle and staring eyeballs awaiting the reappearance of the child.

The dog came up instantly but alone, for the dash over the fall had wrenched the child from his grasp. He looked around eagerly for a moment and then caught sight of a little hand raised above the boiling flood. In one moment he had hold of the child again, and, just as the *prow* of the mother's canoe touched the shore, he brought the child to land.

The mother sprang to the spot, snatched the child from him and gazed in anguish on its deathlike face. Then she laid her cheek on its cold breast and stood motionless. After a few moments she was conscious of some slight movement in the little body and a gentle motion of the hand. The child still lived! Opening up her blanket she drew the covering close around the child, and sitting down on the bank, wept aloud for joy.

Activities

A   Answer these questions. (Answer in sentence form where possible.)

1. How do you know that the current was very strong?
2. Why did the dog not swim with the current when rescuing the child?
3. How can you tell whether the mother's canoe was above or below the fall?
4. What suggests that the dog was (a) very strong, (b) very intelligent?
5. How can you tell from the passage that the dog could act very quickly?
6. Why did the mother herself not rescue the child?
7. Why, in your opinion, did the mother place her cheek on the child's breast?
8. How did she know that the child was still alive?
9. Write another title for the story.
10. Write a paragraph about an accident that happened to you.

B   Write the words in *italics* in interesting sentences of your own.
Look up the words in your dictionary if you're unsure of their meaning.

C   Summarise the story in your own words.
Use about ten sentences.

D   Wordsearch: Dogs. Unscramble the words and find them in the grid.

1. albrorad   _____
2. sapnile   _____
3. ierretr   _____
4. obxre   _____
5. odopel   _____
6. agelbe   _____
7. cloiel   _____
8. eshepgod   _____
9. ttoriwelre   _____
10. itsalaan   _____
11. ckasjusrell   _____
12. rdettsere   _____

s	h	e	e	p	d	o	g	r	s	p	r	a
z	k	g	i	m	j	s	n	d	l	t	o	b
l	a	p	o	o	d	l	e	a	x	e	t	r
l	g	t	q	x	i	r	b	p	i	a	t	e
e	m	h	r	n	o	r	g	l	r	e	w	t
s	k	j	e	g	a	m	l	e	d	s	e	t
s	e	w	x	d	h	o	s	z	p	g	i	e
u	l	r	o	q	c	x	f	a	e	s	l	s
r	g	r	b	n	d	m	n	d	p	q	e	d
k	a	s	s	g	w	i	p	a	h	h	r	e
c	e	p	g	z	e	x	n	t	w	n	l	r
a	b	w	m	l	q	r	e	i	r	r	e	t
j	z	c	n	a	i	t	a	s	l	a	l	a

E   Pretend you lost your pet. Draw an eye-catching poster that you will post on the window in your local shop.

Cloze

A Rewrite the passages using the words from the lists.

neighbour	discovered	fields	country	Africa	sold	found
empire	wearing	years	supplied	capital	wearing	scene

In 1430, the custom of _____ a diamond as a personal ornament began when Agnes Sorel started _____ one in the French court. For the next three hundred _____ , India _____ the diamond demand. In 1725, diamonds were _____ in Brazil and this _____ became the next chief supplier of diamonds. In 1867, in South _____ , a poor farmer's child _____ a pretty stone. A clever _____ recognized it as a diamond, bought it, and when he _____ it, diggers from all over flocked to the _____ . Within a year, three great diamond _____ were found and the city of Kimberley, the _____ of the diamond _____ , was born.

B

searching	immense	exterminate	covered	control	large
sprayed	grow	crops	square	found	

Locusts: These pests are really large grasshoppers, and do _____ damage to _____ on the ground when they gather in _____ swarms. It is even worse when they _____ wings after about 40 days as "hoppers", and fly in huge numbers _____ for food. One East African swarm _____ an area of 250 _____ miles! Scientists have studied the behaviour of locusts, and have _____ that it is best to _____ them at the "hopping" stage with poison on the ground. They are _____ with poison from aircraft, and attacked with flame-throwers. What do you think of this type of locust _____ ?

C

fend	favourite	eaglets	rocky	talons	hooked	kills	feathers
bonnets	goose	claws	small	often	before	because	also	used

An eagle is about the size of a _____ . It has a strong, _____ bill and powerful _____ , or talons. The _____ are used to grasp and hold the _____ animals, snakes and birds which the eagle _____ and eats. The eagle's _____ nesting place is a high, _____ shelf on the side of a mountain. Its nest is called an eyrie and it is _____ the size of a small hut. Baby eagles (_____) are three months old _____ they can fly and _____ for themselves. The Golden Eagle of North America is _____ called the War Eagle, _____ Native American tribes _____ its _____ for their war _____ .

Grammar

> **Capital letters are used for:**
> a) The start of a sentence – My father works very hard.
> b) The names of weekdays, months and festivals – The school is open from Monday to Friday.
> c) The names of people, a title when used with a name, titles of relations when used with actual names – Mary Jones is my friend.
> She shook hands with President McAleese.
> He met his Aunt Mary in town.

 A Rewrite the sentences, putting in the capital letters.

1. last sunday, tom and mary visited aunt jane.
2. last thursday, the school closed and remained closed until monday.
3. joan smith and michael murphy are cousins.
4. good friday and shrove tuesday are dates in the Christian calendar.
5. mary and john brown are my friends in school.
6. mrs singh met mrs prasad.
7. the duke of albany was a very rich man.
8. the queen of england has reigned for a long time.
9. we saw uncle tom's new car.
10. the lecture was given by professor makutsi.

> **Capital letters are used for:**
> a) "I" when used on its own – I do not know why I failed my exam.
> b) The names of places and words made from the names of places. Many French people come to London in the summer.
> c) Titles of books, films, plays – Louis Stevenson wrote "Treasure Island".

 B Rewrite the sentences, putting in the capital letters.

1. my aunt kate travelled from london to paris by train.
2. i ran until i thought i would collapse from exhaustion.
3. thousands of german and french supporters travelled to japan to see the game.
4. shakespeare wrote the play "julius caesar".
5. everybody knows that rio de janeiro is a large city in brazil.
6. they grow oranges in valencia in spain.
7. we went to see the film "shrek 2".
8. the river indus flows through hyderabad.
9. i would like to read "harry potter".
10. the plane flew from kuala lumpur to beijing and then on to tokyo.

Writing

 A **Read the following profile which Laura Brown has written about herself.**

1. Name
    Laura Brown

    Address
    Victoria Lane, York, England

Age	Birthday	
Twelve	5th June	

Height	Weight	Hair	Eyes
1m 57cm	40kg	Brown	Green

Brothers	Sisters	Uncles	Aunts
2	None	6	3

School	Principal	Class Teacher	Pupils
Victoria Secondary	Mrs Booth	Mr Evans	785

2. Friends: My two best friends are Mary Smith and
    Ann Young. Mary is tall and dark, with brown eyes
    and curly hair. Ann is small and fair, with straight hair.
    We play every day and on Saturdays we go swimming
    in the local pool.

3. Likes: Fish and chips, country walks, cats, pop music, nature programmes on TV.

4. Dislikes: Onions, visits to the dentist, mice, boastful people.

5. Hobbies: Cycling is my favourite hobby. I've had a bike for two years and whenever
    the weather is fine I cycle to the country with my friends. I have learned to repair
    punctures and maintain my bike in good condition.

6. Favourite Place: I love the moors where we often go walking at the weekends. I like
    to eat my sandwiches sitting in the bracken, listening to the skylarks singing and
    watching the clouds.

B **Write your own profile, with headings similar to Laura's.**

C **Interview a parent or grandparent and write their profile.**

Language

A   **Rewrite these sentences using the opposites of the words in *italics*.**

1. The sea was very *calm* when the boat *left*.
2. The *old* man walked *slowly down* the road.
3. She *released* the *healthy* pigeon.
4. Every *morning* he watched the sun *rising in the east*.
5. He *bought* the *sweet* grapes at a *high* price.
6. They rowed *slowly* across the *deep* lake.
7. He *ascended* to the *top* of the mountain with great *difficulty*.
8. The *handsome* prince *found* the *bright new* key.
9. The *careful* driver set off at *sunset*.
10. I *seldom* visit my *aunt* in Abu Dhabi.

B   **Rewrite these sentences using the opposites of the words in *italics*.**

1. The *private* house is situated near a *quiet* road.
2. Mary *purchased* a *big black* statue.
3. The *junior* partner in the firm *sold* the house.
4. The *innocent* man was punished by the *coward*.
5. The *small* rats *retreated* along the dusty road.
6. The *miserable man* cried when *he lost his* dog.
7. The *weak woman* lifted the *light* bar over *her* head.
8. The *proud* soldier waited for the train to *arrive*.
9. Joan has a *permanent* job in the *new* factory.
10. The *cheap* case fell on the *poor* man's toe.

C   **Complete and write these sentences.**
The two words in each sentence must be opposite in meaning.
Example: The strawberries were *sweet* but the lemons were *bitter*.

1. He _____ a new bicycle and _____ his old one.
2. I borrowed a book from the pr_____ library as the pub_____ library was closed.
3. The oranges were pl_____ but the prunes were sc_____ .
4. The cats ad_____ along the street but when they saw the dogs they r_____ .
5. The ex_____ of the building was not as beautiful as the in_____ .
6. The main en_____ was guarded by police but I escaped through a side e_____ .
7. The timber was r_____ but the plywood was s_____ .
8. He pleaded i_____ in court but the jury found him g_____ .
9. He dived in at the d_____ end of the pool and swam to the s_____ end.
10. I was lucky to find a v_____ space in the car park and I o_____ it.

Reading

 A   Read the text.

UFOs

Two policemen were in a patrol car on a dark night in October 1967, when they suddenly noticed strange *pulsating* lights in the sky. Soon the lights began to move, skimming swiftly and silently over the tops of trees.

The startled policemen gave chase. Each time they caught up with them, the lights would suddenly accelerate away at *supersonic* speed and then slow down to about 60 kph, allowing the patrol car to catch up again. This game went on for twenty minutes, then the lights suddenly took off up into the skies and vanished. The mysterious object that the policemen had seen is known as a UFO, or an Unidentified Flying Object.

This event took place in England, and it caused a sensation in the newspapers at the time. But similar sightings had been happening for years. Back in 1948, the alarm sirens went off at Fort Knox in the USA when a giant, cone-shaped object was observed hovering in the skies. Four air force planes were immediately sent to investigate. One of the pilots, Captain Thomas Mantell, spotted the UFO and reported, "It's metallic... a tremendous size... it's climbing... I'm going to follow it..." Minutes later his aircraft crashed.

On January 10, 1964, a UFO is reported to have flown across the skies of Cape Kennedy during the firing of a missile. The radar followed the zigzag course of the UFO for fifteen minutes before it got back on the track of the missile. UFOs have also been sighted by astronauts during space missions. It is said that the Apollo 12 moon flight was, for a time, "escorted" by two UFOs, one in front and one following. One astronaut on board remarked that "they were very bright and seemed to be flashing at us".

But the most *baffling* story of all concerns a Brazilian named Antonio Villas Boars. His name first hit the headlines in 1957 when he claimed that he had been kidnapped by aliens and taken on board their spaceship. A doctor who examined Boars said that he was in an extreme state of shock and fear following some terrible *ordeal*. Boars claimed to have been held captive for four and a half hours while the aliens carried out a series of tests on him. Many people do not believe him, but Boars has never changed his story.

What do you think?

Activities

A   Answer these questions.

1.   What does the abbreviation UFO mean?
2.   What were the two policemen doing on the night in question?
3.   What does supersonic mean?
4.   How did the lights play games with the policemen?
5.   In what country did the "lights event" take place?
6.   In what country is Fort Knox?
7.   For how long did the radar follow the course of the UFO?
8.   What did Antonio Villas Boars claim in a newspaper article?
9.   Did Boars ever change his story?
10. Do you believe in UFOs?

B   Write the words in *italics* in interesting sentences of your own.
Look up the words in your dictionary if you're unsure of their meaning.

C   Summarise the story in your own words.
Use about ten sentences.

D   Wordsearch: Body. Find the words in the grid.

1.   spine
2.   shoulder
3.   lungs
4.   heart
5.   fingernail
6.   hair
7.   eyelashes
8.   stomach
9.   kneecap
10. liver
11. skin
12. brain

m	x	s	h	o	u	l	d	e	r
k	z	q	s	w	r	s	j	b	e
e	p	h	c	k	d	p	u	r	y
y	l	k	s	m	i	i	h	a	e
f	i	n	g	e	r	n	a	i	l
h	v	e	n	w	f	e	i	n	a
e	e	e	u	a	a	z	r	k	s
a	r	c	l	t	k	h	m	f	h
r	h	a	a	x	e	d	y	e	e
t	k	p	h	c	a	m	o	t	s

Cloze

A Rewrite the passages using the words from the lists.

treasure	plaited	pistol	reached	coloured	saw	terror	wounds

ship   lighted   huge   body   down   infamous

Blackbeard: The _____ pirate Blackbeard was a _____ savage-looking man with a beard that _____ half way _____ his chest. When going into action he _____ his beard and tied each plait with a _____ ribbon. With _____ tapers stuck in his hat and a _____ in both hands, he must have struck _____ into all who _____ him. He spread terror along the coast of America and stole vast _____ from other ships. He died – with over twenty _____ in his _____ – fighting a _____ of the British Navy.

B

moving   hawk   machine   around   backwards   needed   was   blades

things   real   space   difficult   straight   has   sometimes

Helicopter: A helicopter can do many _____ that an aeroplane cannot. It can fly straight up or _____ down, _____ or sideways. It can hover over one spot, like a _____ in the air, and it can take off or land in a very small _____ .
A helicopter has no wings but it _____ a set of _____ that whirl _____ .
Because of this, it is _____ called a "whirly-bird", and the air _____ over the whirling blades gives the lift _____ to make the _____ fly. The first _____ helicopter flight _____ made in America in 1939. It is a _____ machine to pilot.

C

tied   original   vicious   mast   seven   fury   storm   hatches

frightened   age   coast   produced   had   afterwards   himself   deck

Turner: One of the greatest and most _____ painters was Joseph Turner (1775–1851). At the _____ of sixty _____ , he found _____ on board a steamboat caught in a _____ storm off the English _____ . The _____ passengers scurried below _____ battening down the _____ for safety. But not Turner; he had himself _____ to the ship's _____ so that he could experience the terrible _____ of the _____ ! Not long _____ he _____ a wonderful painting of what he _____ seen – called "Snowstorm: steamboat off a harbour's mouth".

Grammar

A Insert the capital letters where needed.

1. the ship sailed into the harbour.
2. Joel went to eilat on his holidays.
3. The teacher said, "open your books."
4. Paul gave the football to michael.
5. Adeline Yen Mah wrote the book "chinese cinderella".
6. When i reached the river it was in flood.
7. Many people lost their lives when the titanic sank.
8. The river seine flows through paris.
9. I like reading greek legends.
10. The date today is wednesday, 21 july.

B Complete the following sentences using capital letters.

1. Perhaps he is _____ as his father lives in Italy.
2. She is a Parisienne. She comes from _____ and speaks _____ .
3. I am an Athenian. I am from _____ .
4. My friend is from Spain. He is _____ .
5. Maybe he is from _____ as he speaks Portuguese.
6. _____ cheese is manufactured in Denmark.
7. They are Venetians. They come from _____ .
8. When we went to Japan we tried to speak _____ .
9. I am Sven. My home is in Sweden. I speak _____ .
10. The _____ live in Finland and speak _____ .

C Insert the capital letters.

1. we do not go to school on christmas day.
2. muslims all over the world celebrate ramadan.
3. november comes between october and december.
4. muriel's mother made pancakes on shrove tuesday.
5. my summer holidays lasted from june to september.
6. we are going on holiday on the second friday in march.
7. in the united states of america, the fourth of july is called independence day.
8. april the first is called april fools' day.

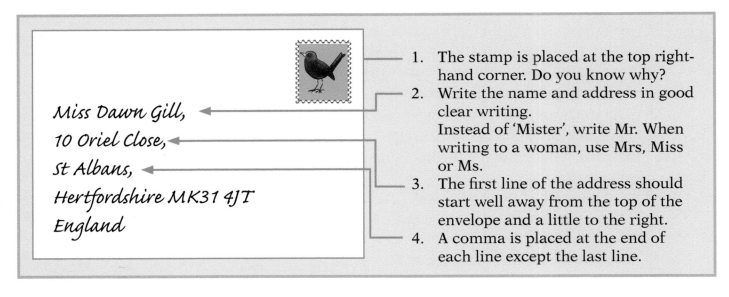

1. The stamp is placed at the top right-hand corner. Do you know why?
2. Write the name and address in good clear writing.
    Instead of 'Mister', write Mr. When writing to a woman, use Mrs, Miss or Ms.
3. The first line of the address should start well away from the top of the envelope and a little to the right.
4. A comma is placed at the end of each line except the last line.

Miss Dawn Gill,
10 Oriel Close,
St Albans,
Hertfordshire MK31 4JT
England

A Write what the abbreviations mean.

Co. _____   Pk _____   Cl. _____

St _____   Gro. _____   Sq. _____

Cres. _____   Ave _____   Tce _____

Rd _____   Dr. _____   Upr _____

B Draw an envelope and address it to yourself.

line 1: name
line 2: street or road
line 3: town
line 4: county and postcode
line 5: country (if letter is being sent abroad)

Language

> **Its or It's**
> a) **Its** – means belonging to something.
>   Example: The horse tossed **its** head in the air and pawed the
>   ground with **its** hooves.
> b) **It's** – means it is or it has.
>   Examples: **It's** a wonderful day. **It's** been raining all night.

A Write the sentences, using **its** or **it's**.

1. _____ spines protects it from _____ enemies.
2. _____ not certain if _____ leg is sprained.
3. _____ a long way to Alaska but _____ worth going there.
4. _____ time to leave but _____ raining heavily.
5. _____ a shame _____ wing is broken.
6. _____ summer and the swallow has returned to _____ nest.
7. _____ been a long time since we visited this art gallery.
8. _____ white tail bobbed up and down as it scurried into _____ burrow.
9. _____ not often we have seen an otter in _____ holt.
10. When _____ winter in Europe _____ summer in Australia.

> **I or Me**
> a) After the verb **to be** use **I**: It was **I** who knocked.
> b) After **prepositions** use **me**: The lion stared at **me**.
> c) After **let** and **between** use **me**: The money was divided between Bill and **me**.

B Write the sentences, using **I** or **me**.

1. She gave _____ a sweet and _____ gave her an orange.
2. Let you and _____ go to the cinema tonight.
3. He pushed _____ and _____ stumbled.
4. Mary and _____ played chess.
5. Mother divided the sweets between Meera and _____ .
6. Halah is older than _____ but _____ am stronger than her.
7. The ball bounced between Tim and _____ but _____ caught it.
8. The angry goat chased _____ and _____ jumped over the ditch.
9. My brother is nearly as tall as _____ .
10. Rory is older than _____ but _____ am younger than Fiona.
11. She is almost as big as _____ .
12. The teacher asked _____ to do the sum on the board and _____ did it.
13. It was _____ who called to see you last night.
14. Do you think it was _____ who stole your pencil?
15. I am certain that it was not _____ who did it.

Read the text.

The Crocodile – An Endangered Species

Experts believe that, unless they are protected, there will be no crocodiles living in the world in a few years time. Crocodiles' habitats have been destroyed by *irrigation* and dam building and many crocodiles have been killed by *poachers*.

Of the twenty-one species of crocodile in the world, fifteen are endangered. The surviving numbers of the species are rapidly declining.

There are 280 Orinoco crocodiles left surviving. There are 11,000 Siamese crocodiles, but none of these are in the wild; they all live on crocodile farms. It is so long since anyone has seen a Chinese crocodile that it is thought to be extinct. Of the Gharial crocodiles, 60 survive in India and 40 in Nepal.

Crocodiles existed 200 million years ago, and survived when the dinosaurs died out. Now they are in danger of becoming extinct because of bad management of the environment and because their skin is sometimes used to make shoes and handbags.

Conservationist studies of crocodiles have discovered some amazing facts. Depending on the species, fully grown crocodiles range in size from one metre to seven and a half metres. They weigh from a few kilograms to well over a tonne. Some estimates say that they can live for 100 years. Crocodiles grunt, hiss, chirp and growl. Each noise carries a message. They also communicate under the water by blowing bubbles. They are cunning enough to track down prey, strong enough to tackle animals as big as a water buffalo and gentle enough to crack open an egg so as not to injure the young inside. Those species of crocodile that live in salt water are the biggest and most dangerous.

The Ancient Egyptians had so much respect for crocodiles that they actually built a whole city, known as Crocodilopolis, for them to live in. Specially chosen priests would enter the city, *adorn* the crocodiles' legs with golden bracelets, open the jaws of *basking* crocodiles and put roasted meat, cakes and wine mixed with honey into their gaping mouths.

Today, a lot of people are only interested in crocodiles for one reason, their valuable hide skin. Manufacturers in Europe and America pay huge prices for crocodile skin. Although strict laws against the sale and purchase of crocodile skin have been enforced worldwide, poaching is still carried out on a large scale. The supply of crocodiles is not endless. If we are not careful, these reptiles, which have lived on this planet longer than humans, will no longer exist.

Activities

A Answer these questions.

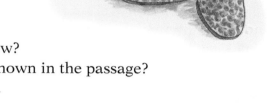

1. How has the crocodile's habitat been destroyed?
2. How many species of crocodile are there?
3. What is the main reason that the crocodile may become extinct?
4. What do crocodiles weigh?
5. How do crocodiles communicate with each other?
6. Where do the most dangerous crocodiles live?
7. What was "Crocodilopolis"?
8. Why does poaching still take place, despite the law?
9. A crocodile can also be very gentle. How is this shown in the passage?
10. Name four other animals in danger of extinction.

B Write the words in *italics* in interesting sentences of your own.
Look up the words in your dictionary if you're unsure of their meaning.

C "Strange". Choose another word for "strange".

surprising	unfamiliar	unusual	haunted	foreign	novel	eccentric	peculiar

1. strange land
2. strange face
3. strange idea
4. strange house
5. strange character
6. strange story
7. strange to say
8. strange writing

D Wordsearch: Wild Animals.
Unscramble the words and find them in the grid.

1. fgiraef _____
2. ioln _____
3. ahceteh _____
4. gallitaro _____
5. occrieldo _____
6. pehletan _____
7. ogriall _____
8. omeso _____
9. rinhcoreso _____
10. mcale _____
11. atnguanro _____
12. adnacona _____

l	i	o	n	r	o	t	a	g	i	l	l	a
p	q	h	d	o	m	k	d	b	b	v	c	l
y	u	a	k	m	y	f	z	r	o	x	e	k
m	g	t	w	b	d	e	f	n	z	m	m	e
a	k	e	n	a	t	u	g	n	a	r	o	f
l	f	e	g	z	h	q	d	c	e	e	o	f
l	q	h	e	e	n	p	r	f	f	g	s	a
i	z	c	r	o	c	o	d	i	l	e	e	r
r	a	n	a	c	o	n	d	a	q	p	p	i
o	w	e	m	t	n	a	h	p	e	l	e	g
g	s	o	r	e	c	o	n	i	h	r	x	w

E Design a badge that you might wear highlighting the need to protect our endangered species.

Cloze

A Write the passage using the words.

> flippers pursued leave species congregate continent inspecting against
> southern mainly series hollow hatch stories replaced result learns
> skin collect helpless look quite two whales land zoos water

Penguins are found _____ around the shores and off-shore islands of the Antarctic _____ . Even though they breed on shore, they are really at home in the _____ , and obtain their food in the sea. Penguins eat fish, squids and small crustaceans. They swim entirely with their _____ , using their feet for steering. With such enemies as sharks, killer _____ and leopard seals, penguins have to be fast. When being _____ by an enemy, penguins sometimes proceed in a _____ of leaps, partly swimming and partly jumping out of the water.

At breeding time, penguins _____ the sea, and large numbers _____ together in the same place year after year. Usually one or _____ eggs are laid in the nest of grass or in a _____ lined with stones. However, there are two _____ which lay only one egg. This egg, which rests on the feet, is covered by a fold of _____ on the lowest part of the body.

When they _____ out, the chicks are covered by a thick down. While one parent goes to the sea to _____ food, the other stays and guards the chick. Soon, the down is _____ by feathers. When this happens, Junior goes to the sea and _____ to swim.

Penguins are quite _____ on land and would be _____ defenceless _____ land enemies. But, in the _____ Polar regions where they live, there are no large _____ animals, with the _____ that they have no fear of anything on land.

Explorers tell _____ of penguins visiting and _____ their camps. Some penguins in _____ become very attached to the people who feed and _____ after them.

B Write the passage using the words.

> period people grasses interesting foraging any when frightening stay
> temperament feed instances believed deepest large awkward declining

When you go to a zoo, one of the most _____ and indeed _____ animals to be seen there is the hippopotamus. These are _____ smooth-skinned mammals that were originally found in the _____ rivers of Africa. They sometimes reach a weight of four tonnes. They have a habit of resting by day and _____ by night. During the day, they _____ on the sandbanks or half-submerged. At night they come out on land to _____ on vegetation, particularly the _____ and reeds along the edges of waters. Even though the hippopotamus looks very _____ when moving on land, it can actually gallop _____ necessary. The hippo is much hunted for its fat, flesh and hide, and in some areas of the world, their numbers are _____ rapidly. In conditions of captivity, the hippo can live for up to a _____ of 50 years. Generally, the hippo is _____ to have a placid _____ , but there are many _____ of attacks by hippos on _____ , and it certainly would not be advisable to take _____ chances with them.

Grammar

A **noun** is a name word. It names some **person, place, animal** or **thing**.
Example: A **pack** of **dogs** frightened the **sheep** in the **field**.
Kim and **Leanne** ate **pancakes** with their **friends**.

  Rewrite this paragraph and underline the nouns.

It was a glorious September day, with the warm sun shining brightly in the blue sky. High up in the air, the lark was filling the heavens with melody, and from tree and hedge came the sweet notes of thrush, blackbird and robin. The sheep were lying peacefully in the shade of the trees, and the horses were knee-deep in the river. Down in the valley, the machines were noisily cutting the golden corn; but louder than the noise of the machines were the shouts of the children, bathing in the cool pool by the ash grove.

B **Write the plurals of these nouns. Use a dictionary if you're unsure.**

Singular	Plural	Singular	Plural	Singular	Plural
branch	_____	salmon	_____	buffalo	_____
face	_____	child	_____	ox	_____
nose	_____	tooth	_____	deer	_____
penny	_____	cargo	_____	chief	_____
army	_____	hero	_____	hoof	_____
cry	_____	echo	_____	piano	_____
flea	_____	dwarf	_____	man	_____
thief	_____	fly	_____	grotto	_____
roof	_____	wolf	_____	cod	_____
potato	_____	goose	_____	sheep	_____
woman	_____	foot	_____	volcano	_____

C **Write the missing nouns.**

> open   night   rodents   tail   crops   now   anything   considered
> common   day   diseases   world

House mice are small, brown-grey _____ with a pointed snout, large ears and a long _____ . They are nocturnal animals, which means they are active at _____ and sleep during the _____ . Originally from Asia, they are _____ found all over the _____ . One of the most _____ land-based mammals after humans, house mice are found in areas where people live and also in _____ fields. House mice will eat almost _____ . Because of their liking for cereal _____ and the fact that they carry several _____ that can be caught by humans, they are often _____ a pest.

Writing

A Write a story called *Marooned On a Desert Island*.
Use the help words and phrases.

shipwrecked in a hurricane
raft   washed ashore
explored island   built hut
gathering coconuts and berries
made weapons
hunting and fishing   loneliness
lit beacon fires   red sail on horizon

B Write a story called *A Strange Dream I Had*.
Use the help words and phrases.

journey to a strange land
tired and weary   deep sleep
army of little people
worked furiously   tied down
struggling to break free
flight of the "little people"
awoke from dream

C Write a story called *A Chariot Race in Ancient Rome*.
Use the help words and phrases.

packed with people   fanfare of trumpets   parade of chariots   starting signal
great roar of excitement   neck and neck   terrible collision
one charioteer forges ahead   carried shoulder high

Language

A Choose an appropriate verb to fill in the blank spaces in the following sentences.

1. The cornered fox _____ fiercely.
2. The old engine _____ noisily up the hill.
3. The hungry baby _____ all night long.
4. The rabbit _____ with terror as the trap _____ on his forelegs.
5. The horses _____ through the swollen river.
6. The huge wave _____ against the rocks.
7. The windows _____ loudly in the violent storm.
8. The explorers _____ slowly through the marshy ground.
9. The cat _____ from her basket by the fire when she _____ the mouse.
10. The alarm bell _____ the sailors from their sleeping cabins.
11. Slowly he _____ his way through the dense undergrowth.
12. The car _____ in order to avoid knocking down the pedestrian.

B Choose an appropriate adjective from the given list to describe each of the birds and then finish the sentence.

proud	tireless	tiny	gentle	little	graceful	swift	tawny

1. The _____ robin hopped from _____ .
2. The _____ owl flitted across _____ .
3. The _____ lark soared high in _____ .
4. The _____ blackbird flew into _____ .
5. The _____ eagle swooped down _____ .
6. The _____ swan flapped her wings when _____ .
7. The _____ seagull glided towards _____ .
8. The _____ wren hopped along _____ .

C Fill in the blank spaces in the following sentences with **was** or **were**.

1. My mother _____ in hospital and my sisters _____ in school.
2. Her dress _____ black and her shoes _____ white.
3. The stockings _____ red and the coat _____ brown.
4. You _____ in Paris when she _____ in London.
5. She _____ wrong and you _____ right.
6. They _____ cycling but Mary _____ walking.
7. She _____ frightened but I _____ not.
8. The boy _____ crying but his friends _____ laughing.
9. Her gloves _____ stolen when she _____ at the dance.
10. It _____ night and we _____ far from home.

Reading

A Read the text.

Plant Survival

Plants first appeared on earth 400 million years ago. Insects arrived 100 million years later. Ever since, a fierce war has raged between the two.

At first it does not seem likely that the plants would stand any chance in the battle. Plants, unlike insects, cannot move. Plants are vastly outnumbered by insects; an *average* oak tree will have tens of thousands of insects feeding on it. The great *naturalist* Charles Darwin once carried out an interesting experiment to show how insects destroy plants. He dug and cleared a piece of ground about one metre square and then began counting all the tiny weeds as they sprang out of the earth. Out of the 357 plants that grew, 295 were destroyed by insects.

However, despite this fierce *onslaught*, plants are well able to survive. Scientists now know that plants have been using deadly chemicals and poison gas to *deter* their enemies! One type of potato releases a chemical that will kill any greenfly attacking it. Tomatoes can release a gas

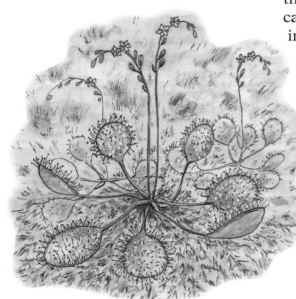

that kills attacking worms. Trees produce a poison called tannin when their leaves are chewed by hungry insects. Perhaps the most amazing defence of all is that used by the bracken plant. It will produce cyanide, the most deadly of all poisons, when the chewing insects attack. But bracken does allow ants to drink its nectar; the ants, in return, fight off other insects that attack the plant.

A small group of plants has launched a full-scale *offensive* against their enemies in this great war. These are the *carnivorous* plants. They have turned to trapping, killing and devouring insects.

Activities

A   Answer these questions.

1. When did plants first appear?
2. What advantages have insects in this "war"?
3. Who was Charles Darwin?
4. What "weapons" do plants use to defend themselves?
5. What did Darwin's experiment show?
6. When does the bracken plant produce cyanide?
7. Why are ants not poisoned by bracken?
8. What is a carnivorous plant?

B   Write the words in *italics* in interesting sentences of your own.
Look up the words in your dictionary if you're unsure of their meaning.

C   Write the opposite of the words in *italics*.

1. *Summer* days are *long* and *warm*.
2. The girl was *laughing* because she was *happy*.
3. The boy swam in the *shallow* pool.
4. The *wet* sand was *soft* under my feet.
5. *Late* one *evening* the swallows flew *southwards*.
6. The *old* lady walked along the *narrow* path.
7. The boy is *tall* and *fat*.
8. The aeroplane flew *above* the *white* clouds.

D   Wordsearch: Plants and Insects.
Unscramble the words and find
them in the grid.

1. ebe   _____
2. swpa   _____
3. efal   _____
4. tnetel   _____
5. ebteel   _____
6. dersip   _____
7. yscameor   _____
8. erflbuytt   _____
9. rgass   _____
10. wolref   _____
11. nat   _____

p	b	c	d	d	f	x	b	a	g	g	z	p
d	d	e	p	h	r	e	s	m	n	n	b	e
u	g	p	h	x	e	e	d	p	r	f	e	b
w	g	b	k	t	w	a	a	n	y	b	f	u
d	p	a	l	t	g	p	s	a	w	x	d	t
c	d	e	f	r	w	x	n	c	d	p	o	t
e	k	b	a	t	n	a	g	w	h	p	r	e
r	k	s	m	o	p	b	c	g	f	d	r	r
o	s	x	h	d	e	l	t	t	e	n	e	f
m	a	w	f	s	p	i	d	e	r	k	w	l
a	z	k	p	p	t	x	w	u	p	d	o	y
c	a	a	e	l	f	y	t	t	k	b	l	e
y	y	h	c	a	d	r	k	c	d	c	f	g
s	k	m	p	d	h	w	z	d	b	c	a	w

E   One word should not have appeared in the wordsearch.
Which one and why?

Cloze

A Write the passage using the words.

bounced	bounces	still	ordinary	hear	short	least	from
	shout	echo	high	might	reflects	waves	

Echoes: As sound travels, it hits things in its path and _____ back just as a ball _____ bounce. An echo is made by the return of the sound _____ to your ear. When you _____ in a large yard with a _____ wall, you hear your own voice _____ back at you _____ the wall. In _____ rooms sound bounces off the walls, but the trip is so _____ and fast that the _____ occurs while you are _____ speaking. You can only _____ an echo if you are at _____ 18 metres away from the surface that _____ the sound.

B Write the passage using the words.

distance	distances	nearest	revolve	does	during	have	less	about

Is the Moon always the same distance from the Earth? The Moon _____ not _____ around the Earth in a circle, but in an ellipse. It is, therefore, not always the same _____ from the Earth. At its farthest point it is _____ 404,800 km away, and at its _____ about 355,200 km. Astronauts _____ to take these _____ into account _____ a journey to the Moon because each kilometre _____ means a saving in fuel.

C Write the passage using the words.

could	violent	away	almost	far	covered	sunset	noise
			heard	globe			

Krakatoa: The eruption of the Krakatoa volcano in 1883 was so _____ that the _____ could be _____ over 4,000 km _____ in Bangkok. The dust from the eruption _____ _____ every part of the _____ , and for the next two years it formed a thin haze which _____ be seen in the sky at _____ , in places as _____ away as Dublin.

Grammar

Kinds of Nouns
a) A **proper noun** is the special name given to one particular person, place or thing that you wish to distinguish in a special way. These nouns are always written with a capital letter.
Example: **John**, **Hong Kong**, **SS Titanic**, **Friday**, **King Kong**.
b) A **common noun** denotes no one person or thing, but is common to all persons or things of the same kind.
Example: **man**, **country**, **boy**, **chair**, **pencil**, **woman**.
c) A **collective** noun is the name of a group, collection of persons or things, considered as one complete whole.
Example: **herd**, **crowd**, **swarm**, **pack**.
d) An **abstract noun** is the name of a quality, feeling or idea. It relates to things which cannot be seen, touched, felt or tasted. It is not associated with any object or objects.
Example: **poverty**, **health**, **height**, **revenge**, **flight**, **love**, **charity**.

A   Write the nouns from each sentence.
Write whether they are **proper**, **common**, **collective** or **abstract**.

1. Yasmin and Rajan went to the seaside.
2. Greece is a country in Europe.
3. She is a woman of great intelligence.
4. The chain was made of gold.
5. The dog likes to eat meat and chew bones.
6. The depth of the river was no problem to the diver.
7. Tom uses a tractor when ploughing, but John uses a team of horses.
8. He managed to escape under the cover of darkness.
9. Honesty is the best policy.
10. A plague of locusts ate all the wheat.
11. The boy chopped wood for the fire.
12. She travelled to Budapest by train.
13. Rabbits eat grass but otters eat fish.
14. We breathe air into our lungs.
15. The fisherman filled his basket with fish.
16. A pack of hungry dogs attacked the sheep.
17. The owner of the hotel is a friendly person.
18. Femi kept her pet parrot in a cage.
19. The ship struck a reef but the crew was saved.
20. Many people around the world are working tirelessly for peace.
21. It gave me great pleasure to introduce the speaker.
22. She witnessed the collision of two trains.
23. The floor was slippery.
24. I could see the anxiety in his face.
25. Scrooge lived his life in misery.

Writing

A proofreader is someone who checks that a piece of writing has no mistakes. One of the things they check for is spelling.

A Proofread this letter from the Troll to the Billy Goats Gruff. Write the letter correctly.

The Troll,
Room 5,
Ward 1048,
Troll Hospitle.

5 Septembre

Dear Goats,
As you can sea I'm writing to yo from my hospitel bed. I hope you're all happy, now that you've finelly got fid of me. Well you havn't got rid of me, becus I'll bee back. Ass I evur wanted wuz for us to bee frens. But what did I get for my trubble? A terubul thumping. Nun of the other trolls can beleeve how horribel you wear to me. They all get on very well with there goats. Annyweigh like I sed, I'll be back. I shud warn you that I'll be bringing an armee of trolls with mee. I'm not going to take this lying down. Its time for me to fight bac.

Yours sinseerlee,
Troll.

B The handsome prince is desperate to find Cinderella. He decides to put an advertisement in the newspaper. He can only use 15 words. Write an advertisement for him. (Remember he has the slipper.)

C Red Riding Hood is sick of wearing the same old clothes. She wants a "new" image. Design a new outfit for her. Describe it for Granny who can't see very well.

D Do you remember the story of "The Ugly Duckling"? Can you re-tell the story using just one paragraph?

E Write a different ending for your favourite fairy tale.

Language

 A Write another word for "said". The words are scrambled.

1. ddade _____
2. madittde _____
3. avisdde _____
4. gradee _____
5. snaerwed _____
6. stboaed _____
7. ragbgde _____
8. mocplinaed _____
9. carledde _____
10. eqnuider _____

11. torpetsed _____
12. makrrede _____
13. ortreted _____
14. sghide _____
15. eensder _____
16. gestgused _____
17. nwarde _____
18. lleyed _____
19. oarred _____
20. finomred _____

21. mgrubedl _____
22. clexaiedm _____
23. plexanied _____
24. feconseds _____
25. wishpeder _____
26. asnrlde _____
27. ttmueder _____
28. amoedn _____
29. urmedurm _____
30. wgorlde _____

 B Write these sentences, using another word for **said** from the list.

| jeered | asked | ordered | groaned | begged | grumbled | demanded |
| shouted | whispered | answered |

1. "The pain in my shoulder is getting worse," *said* Abid.
2. "Your bike is not as good as mine," *said* Lin.
3. "The teacher gives us too much homework," *said* Tim.
4. "Can you swim four lengths of the pool?" *said* Paul.
5. "I can easily swim four lengths," *said* Mary.
6. "There is to be no talking during fire-drill," *said* the teacher.
7. "Please take us to the circus," *said* the children.
8. "I want my money back," *said* the customer.
9. "Don't make a sound or they will hear us," *said* Baldev.
10. "If you do not behave yourself, I will order you off," *said* the referee.

 C Write these sentences, using another word for **said**.

1. "Where is the pop concert being staged?" Andrew *said*.
2. The manager *said*, "The show is about to commence."
3. "I did not break the window," *said* James.
4. "Good gracious!" *said* the lady, "I have lost my purse."
5. "My leg is wedged between the boulders," *said* the injured man.
6. "Don't make a sound," *said* Mr. Reilly, "the baby is asleep."
7. "I am going to win first prize," *said* Sahira.
8. "I work long hours and you pay me little money," *said* the worker.
9. "What a beautiful view!" *said* the tourist.

A Read the text.

The Grand Canyon

A canyon is a steep-sided valley cut by a river. The Grand Canyon in the state of Arizona in the United States of America is one of the most spectacular canyons in the world. It is 446 kilometres long and about 1.6 kilometres deep. Its width varies *significantly*, from just over a kilometre in some places, to over 29 kilometres in others.

The Grand Canyon has been forming gradually over the last six million years, as the Colorado River has cut through *successive* layers of soft rock, including limestone, sandstone and shale. The different layers vary in colour, and they all change shade during the course of a day, as the light changes. At sunset the red and brown layers look particularly strongly coloured.

The Grand Canyon has its own unique *climate*. The further down the canyon you go, the hotter and drier it becomes. Amazingly, temperatures at the bottom can be up to 14 degrees Celsius higher than at the top, and the average annual rainfall at the bottom is about a quarter of the rainfall at the top.

This wide range of weather patterns makes the Grand Canyon an ideal *habitat* for many different types of plants and animals. There are about 300 species of birds alone, and about 120 other species of animals, including beavers, bighorn sheep, elk, lizards, mountain lions and snakes. Grand Canyon rattlesnakes aren't found anywhere else in the world.

On the rim of the canyon there are a lot of ponderosa pine trees. On the south side, juniper and pinon pines grow in lower areas. Aspen, fir, and spruce live at the highest levels in the north. Cactuses grow throughout the canyon area, and are especially common in low areas.

Various Native American tribes have lived in the Grand Canyon area for the last four thousand years. Today, about 300 members of the Havasupai tribe live in a side canyon called Havasu Canyon.

The first Europeans to see the Grand Canyon, in 1540, were a group of Spanish explorers led by Garcia Lopez de Cardenas. The canyon wasn't given its current name until 1869, when the American geologist John Wesley Powell became the first person of European descent to lead a river expedition through the vast canyon.

In 1919, Grand Canyon National Park was *established*. The park is dedicated to preserving this natural wonder of the world, and protecting the plants and animals that live there.

Activities

A   **Answer these questions.**

1. Where is the Grand Canyon?
2. How long is the Grand Canyon?
3. Explain how the Grand Canyon has formed.
4. Why is the climate of the Grand Canyon unusual?
5. For about how long have Native American people lived in the area of the Grand Canyon?
6. Where did the first European people to see the canyon come from?
7. Who gave the Grand Canyon its name?
8. What is the purpose of the Grand Canyon National Park?
9. Describe where you would go if you were an explorer.
10. Suggest another title for the text.

B   **Write the words in *italics* in interesting sentences of your own. Look up the words in your dictionary if you're unsure of their meaning.**

C   **Summarise the story in your own words and in about ten sentences.**

Wordsearch: The circus.
Unscramble the words and find them in the grid.

1. etezrap   _____
2. agimanci   _____
3. snowcl   _____
4. rife ertea   _____
5. glerjug   _____
6. ghttipero   _____
7. igb tpo   _____
8. abatcro   _____
9. swastdu   _____
10. hte grin   _____

j	u	g	g	l	e	r	t	l	f
a	b	i	g	t	o	p	i	a	i
y	t	t	s	t	t	s	g	m	r
c	h	a	p	r	l	a	h	k	e
l	e	b	l	a	r	w	t	n	e
o	r	o	l	p	e	d	r	d	a
w	i	r	n	e	p	u	o	j	t
n	n	c	g	z	d	s	p	y	e
s	g	a	u	e	m	t	e	e	r
m	a	g	i	c	i	a	n	a	g

Cloze

A   Write the passage using the words.

over	farmer	little	which	upon	there	realised	off
approaching	choice	distance	dropped	crouched	lazy	where	

Once _____ a time, a donkey ran away from his
master. He trotted into the woods, and _____ found
a lion's skin.

"What a great find," brayed the donkey. He _____ the
skin _____ his back, so that from a _____ he
looked like a lion. All the _____ animals in the wood
ran home and _____ down in fright.

The donkey grew _____ . "I will roar like a lion
and then I can go _____ I like and get all the
_____ food for myself"

But all he could do was bray loudly, and the animals
_____ they had been tricked. The hare ran
_____ and told the farmer where he would find
his lazy ass.

The _____ set off for the wood, and _____ the donkey, grabbed him by his
long ears _____ were sticking through the lion's skin.

"Once an ass, always an ass!" growled the farmer and led him back to his stable.

B   Write the passage using the words.

carried	kind	talons	indifferent	mimic	caught	children
shepherd	unable	large	as	swoop	trapped	got	could	along
himself	an	for	Moreover	thick	flew	needless		

The Eagle and the Daw

Once, a hungry eagle made a _____ at a small lamb, grabbed the little animal in
its _____ and _____ off to its eyrie.

A foolish jackdaw, who tried to _____ everything he saw, attacked a _____
ram just _____ he had seen the eagle do.

The jackdaw tugged and tugged at the _____ ram, but _____ to say,
_____ not move him. _____ , his claws _____ entangled in the ram's
_____ fleece and he got himself _____ and _____ to move!

That evening, the shepherd came _____ and _____ him. The man clipped
his wings and _____ him home as a plaything for his children.

The _____ were delighted. "What _____ of bird is this?" they asked.

"Well, my dears," said the _____ . "He will tell you _____ that he is
_____ eagle, but you can take my word _____ it that he is a daw!"

Grammar

The **apostrophe** is used to show possession or ownership. It avoids the over-use of the word "of" or the words "belonging to". We insert an apostrophe (') before or after the letter **s**.

Rules

(i) We generally use an apostrophe before the letter s ('s) to show that something belongs to one person.
Examples: the girl's hat ... means ... the hat of the girl.
the boy's school ... means ... the school of the boy.

(ii) We generally use an apostrophe after the letter s (s') to show that something belongs to several people.
Examples: the girls' hats ... means the hats of the girls
the boys' school ... means ... the school of the boys

(iii) If the plural of the word does not end in s we add 's to denote possession.
Examples: the mice's cheese ... means ... the cheese of the mice
the men's hats ... means ... the hats of the men

(iv) If the word already ends in s or a sound like s, we either: (a) place the apostrophe after the s or the s sound or else (b) we add 's to form an extra syllable in order to make it easy for us to pronounce the word. Usage of words is the best guideline to follow here.
Examples: (a) for goodness' sake, Moses' people, for conscience' sake, the Times' editor.
(b) James's Street, Jones's Road, Charles's death.

A Rewrite the following sentences using an apostrophe to replace the words in italics.

1. The *rays of the sun* shone on the *surface of the water*.
2. The *hooves of the horse* were cut and bruised by the sharp cobbled stones.
3. She bought an electric guitar in *the shop belonging to her cousin*.
4. The *recreation hall for teenagers* was badly damaged by fire.
5. At the jumble sale the ladies sold several *cardigans for men*.
6. The *names of the two players* were reported to the referee.
7. They sell beautiful toys and clothes in the *department for infants*.
8. It seems that the *sails of the boat* were smashed in the storm.

B Rewrite the sentences, inserting the apostrophe where needed.

1. The police officers helmet lay on the table.
2. Mansas friends arrived at the door.
3. Mr Murphys cat and Mrs Brownes dog were killed last week.
4. The ladies shoes and the referees coat were stolen.
5. Johns friend is staying at his uncles cottage in the country.
6. Mens hats and boys shoes are sold in that shop.
7. The pupils classroom is bigger than the teachers staff room.
8. In the minds eye, the poet still saw the childs beautiful face.

31

Writing

Sometimes we use a shortened version of a word.
Example: phone (telephone) panto (pantomime) you're (you are)
(Note: an apostrophe (') is placed where a letter or letters have been left out).

A Rewrite the full word(s) for these contractions.

1. prom ＿＿＿＿＿
2. phone ＿＿＿＿＿
3. photo ＿＿＿＿＿
4. specs ＿＿＿＿＿
5. mag ＿＿＿＿＿
6. plane ＿＿＿＿＿
7. keeper ＿＿＿＿＿
8. budgie ＿＿＿＿＿
9. tele ＿＿＿＿＿
10. gym ＿＿＿＿＿

11. he's ＿＿＿＿＿
12. he'd ＿＿＿＿＿
13. she'll ＿＿＿＿＿
14. you're ＿＿＿＿＿
15. we're ＿＿＿＿＿
16. what's ＿＿＿＿＿
17. can't ＿＿＿＿＿
18. don't ＿＿＿＿＿
19. you'll ＿＿＿＿＿
20. couldn't ＿＿＿＿＿

B Rewrite the sentences using contractions.

1. I *shall not* be able to go to the concert.
2. It is cold outside and *it is* raining heavily.
3. She *did not* know the correct address.
4. *He is* the tallest boy in the class.
5. *I am* sure *he will* come this evening.
6. *That is* the girl *who is* acting in the play.
7. *We are* going to visit our aunt's house.

C Rewrite these sentences putting in an apostrophe where a letter or letters have been omitted.

1. Dont forget to come early to the party.
2. Shes got the fastest motorbike Ive ever seen.
3. He doesnt know wholl be at the school drama tonight.
4. Theyll be late coming, so lets not wait.
5. Theres a ship I havent seen before in the harbour.
6. Id like to go to the play but Ive got no money.
7. Were all going to the end of term party.
8. If it isnt raining this evening, well go for a walk in the park.
9. We arent ready yet for the dance.
10. Whats the matter?

Language

A noun can be one of four genders.
A noun denoting a male is of masculine gender.
A noun denoting a female is of feminine gender.
A noun denoting either sex is of common gender.
A noun denoting neither sex is of neutral gender.

Examples:
man, prince
woman, princess
child, sheep
wall, box

A Write out these lists.
Write **f**, **m**, **c** or **n** after each word to show the gender.

1. woman _____
2. man _____
3. boy _____
4. girl _____
5. infant _____
6. table _____
7. bird _____
8. mare _____
9. donkey _____
10. aunt _____

11. heroine _____
12. huntress _____
13. stone _____
14. stallion _____
15. mother _____
16. prince _____
17. dress _____
18. cage _____
19. mouse _____
20. ship _____

21. father _____
22. page _____
23. teacher _____
24. hostess _____
25. nephew _____
26. ewe _____
27. floor _____
28. brother _____
29. thief _____
30. niece _____

B Rewrite the sentences, writing the masculine of the words in *italics*.

1. The *shepherdess* gave *Frances* a present of a *ewe*.
2. The *heroine* rescued the *landlady* from the *giantess*.
3. The *duck* and the *goose* attacked the *girl*.
4. The *manageress* ordered the *waitress* to serve the *lady*.
5. The *hostess* and *her daughter* welcomed the *duchess*.
6. The *lioness* killed the *hen*.
7. The *princess* spoke to the *mayoress*.
8. The *spinster* visited the *abbess*.
9. The *actress* and the *stewardess* spoke to the *empress*.
10. *Josephine's grandmother* was once a *governess*.

C Rewrite the sentences, changing the masculines into feminines.

1. The instructor is my brother.
2. The master is my father.
3. The ram attacked the boy.
4. The mayor talked to the group of gentlemen.
5. The heir to the estate had three sons.
6. The king leads his army into battle.
7. His nephew married in Rome last week.
8. The waiter served his father-in-law.
9. The stag ran through the forest.
10. The traitor betrayed his country.

Reading

A Read the story.

The Robin

The robin was now *exceptionally* tame, and never hesitated to come into the house and onto my knee or hand. He appeared on the doorstep about nine o'clock each morning, and would sing in his unmistakable *strident* tones for breakfast. One morning I heard an unusually loud burst of song from him. There he was, inside the front room, perched on top of a clock before a large mirror and singing his loudest at his own reflection, the feathers on the crest of his head raised in obvious anger. But he did not attack the reflection in the two or three minutes I watched him. Before many days, he had investigated every room on the ground floor.

The different notes he produced interested me. His loud *aggressive* song was very *familiar*, but often when he was feeding from my hand or knee, a number of cheeky sparrows would approach enviously, and immediately he would utter angry tic-tic-tic. Then again, if I made any sudden movement while he was on my knee, he would jump about a foot into the air, utter a sharp squeak and hover with rapidly beating wings like a tiny helicopter, before returning to my knee.

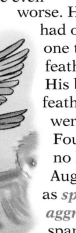

At the end of July, he was *moulting* and, in contrast to his usually *immaculate* appearance, was *bedraggled*. After another week, his appearance had become even worse. He had only one tail feather left. His breast feathers were still more bedraggled and of a dull shade of red. Four days later he was completely without a tail and no longer came up to the house. By the middle of August, however, he had a brand new tail and was as *spruce* as ever. His self-confidence and natural *aggressiveness* returned and he again chased away any sparrows that dared to come near.

Activities

A   Answer these questions.

1. How, in your opinion, did the robin know when to come for his breakfast?
2. In what ways did the robin show his exceptional tameness?
3. "One morning, I heard an unusually loud burst of song." What caused the robin to sing so loudly on that occasion?
4. Why should the sparrows be envious?
5. "He no longer came up to the house." Why not?
6. If you did not understand the word "moulting", you could make out its meaning from the paragraph. Explain how.
7. Write down words which have the same meaning as the following: reflection, investigated, produced, cheeky, self-confidence.
8. Give one word having the opposite meaning of each of the following: tame, different, loud, aggressive, approach.

B   Write the words in *italics* in interesting sentences of your own. Look up the words in your dictionary if you're unsure of their meaning.

C   Summarise the story in your own words and in about ten sentences.

D   Wordsearch: Birds. Unscramble the words and find them in the grid.

a	x	w	k	g	e	p	h	s	u	r	h	t
a	p	d	d	a	h	f	f	w	z	p	p	x
l	g	w	g	p	p	q	a	b	r	f	g	g
u	l	l	r	s	t	h	h	o	b	d	d	w
n	e	k	p	n	w	c	b	r	p	b	d	o
r	c	t	e	h	o	i	l	p	x	w	k	l
e	n	r	p	k	n	w	t	c	l	r	l	l
t	w	m	w	b	h	c	l	k	m	a	q	a
t	b	a	w	l	t	d	g	f	r	g	p	w
i	h	k	o	z	k	p	g	k	e	d	g	s
b	s	a	r	y	w	o	r	r	a	p	s	h
w	p	p	c	y	l	l	u	g	a	e	s	r

1. alswowl   _____
2. rstuhh   _____
3. esallug   _____
4. pwosrra   _____
5. binor   _____
6. elgae   _____
7. arkl   _____
8. low   _____
9. ewrn   _____
10. ahwk   _____
11. rocw   _____
12. itbtenr   _____

E   Write out a list of birds that you have seen in real life (not in books or on TV.)

Phonics

A All the words begin with **B**. Write the answers.

1. The written life of a person. _____
2. The ridge over the eyes. _____
3. The rounded stem or shoot of an onion. _____
4. A writing-desk. _____
5. The name of the bear in Jungle Book. _____
6. A farmer's store house. _____
7. Perfect happiness. _____
8. To cut in halves. _____
9. A million million. _____
10. The science of life. _____
11. A place to sleep in a ship. _____
12. A drone is one. _____

B All the words begin with **H**. Write the answers.

1. A European country. _____
2. This animal has spines for defence. _____
3. A small piece of cloth. _____
4. Very unpleasant. _____
5. The study of coats of arms. _____
6. A plant used for flavouring. _____
7. A large shed where aircraft are kept. _____
8. A mouth organ. _____
9. A floor of or near a fireplace. _____
10. A river-horse. _____
11. A flat shape with six sides. _____
12. With an empty space inside. _____

C There is only one correct spelling in each line.
Can you write the correct spelling of the other two.

1. strech, fractur, fourth _____
2. imposible, jostel, journey _____
3. laughtir, luxery, monthly _____
4. Arctic, Olympick, piller _____
5. rowdey, scoop, shortin _____
6. slippery, steadey, startel _____
7. vacume, voluntery, wafer _____
8. sheikh, beleive, recieve _____
9. populer, postege, porridge _____
10. commotion, caskit, biscuite. _____

Grammar

> **Pronouns** are small words which take the place of nouns.
> Example: The boy read the book. **He** read **it** from cover to cover.

Other pronouns

him	we	them	yours	these	those
any	us	theirs	this	which	whose
some	you	ours	that	who	whom

 A   Rewrite this passage and underline the pronouns.

"It is time for me to know you now. You are abusive and cantankerous like all pampered pets. You forget the times I have saved you from the cat, who will some day kill you. Next time I see her stalking you I will leave you to your fate. And when any strange mongrels or pups visit the house I will not hang around like I do. Good day to you," remarked Fido to his friend Mrs Rabbit.

B   Write the sentences with the correct pronouns.

1. Joan and (*me*, *I*) went for a walk.
2. Who is there? It is (*us*, *we*).
3. Give (*her*, *she*) the money.
4. The dog chased (*him*, *he*) and (*I*, *me*).
5. He invited John and (*me*, *I*) into the shop.
6. The flood prevented (*them*, *they*) from proceeding.
7. It seems to be (*he*, *him*).
8. Is that (*she*, *her*) in that blue hat?
9. He gave (*them*, *they*) to (*him*, *he*).
10. He saw (*us*, *we*) in the street.
11. It now appears it was (*he*, *him*).
12. She was certain it was (*they*, *them*).

 C   Use the pronoun **who** to make ten sentences out of these statements.

1. The passenger left Paris airport at six. She arrived in Rome an hour later.
2. The man brought the cake. He is in the kitchen.
3. The police officer rescued the old man. She was awarded a medal for bravery.
4. The boy stole the apples. He was caught by the gardener.
5. The politician appeared on television. She defended the government.
6. The child ran across the road. He was knocked down by a car.
7. The girl trained every day. She won the gold medal.
8. The surgeon did the operation. He spoke to the patient that evening.
9. The little boy lost his schoolbag. He was crying in the yard.
10. The centre forward scored the goal. He was congratulated by his captain.

Writing

Sea View Hotel,
7 High Street,
Port Macquarie,
New South Wales

3 June 2006

Dear Mum and Dad,

A thousand thanks for your welcome letter which I received this morning. I was excited when I saw it lying on the table. You have no idea how thrilled I was to receive the money. It felt like it was my birthday.

I am delighted to know that you are all well at home. Mary and I are having a wonderful time here in Port Macquarie. The weather is glorious, the people are kind and the food in this hotel is excellent. We are both learning to sail and go swimming every day.

Tell Tom that I'll write to him tomorrow. Remind him to feed Bonzo regularly. I miss you all. Give my love to May and Dan.

Your loving son,
Karl

A   Write a short letter to a friend, inviting him or her to your birthday party.

B   You are on holiday with your aunt. Write a letter home.

C   A friend has left your school. Write a letter telling him or her all the latest news.

D   Write a letter to a famous person inviting him or her to visit your school. The message should contain three paragraphs. (See the three points below.)

1.   Introduce yourself. Describe your school. Explain why you are writing the letter.

2.   Write about why you like this person. What's impressed you about him or her? Why should he or she come to your school?

3.   Closing paragraph: Wish the person well. Indicate that you'll be looking forward to a reply. The ending should indicate your sincerity, for example, Yours sincerely.

Language

A   Write two words that start with each of these prefixes.

1. com _____
2. de _____
3. dis _____
4. ex _____
5. in _____

6. im _____
7. il _____
8. pre _____
9. tele _____
10. un _____

11. bi _____
12. inter _____
13. sub _____
14. post _____
15. re _____

B   Write the sentences using words with the prefix **un**.

1. The warning sign declared that it was un_____ to swim near the rock.
2. He un_____ the door and unleashed the alsatian dog.
3. Mrs Smith's electricity was disconnected because her bill was un_____ .
4. The injured player was un_____ to continue playing.
5. People who are un_____ are not loyal.
6. The patient was un_____ after falling from the ladder.
7. At the inquiry, many facts previously un_____ were revealed.
8. Helen was un_____ to fall and break her leg.
9. The ship's cargo was un_____ .
10. The tyrant king imposed un_____ taxes on the people.
11. We had to rise at an un_____ hour.
12. The un_____ spectators disrupted the game.

C   Write the opposite of these words by using a prefix.

1. correct _____
2. obey _____
3. selfish _____
4. advantage _____
5. patient _____

6. content _____
7. polite _____
8. loyal _____
9. order _____
10. happy _____

11. aware _____
12. pure _____
13. direct _____
14. modest _____
15. lock _____

D   **Trans** means across. Write the meanings of these prefixes.

1. bi _____
2. ex _____
3. ante _____

4. post _____
5. inter _____
6. sub _____

7. com _____
8. ob _____
9. pre _____

Reading

 Read the text.

The Sun King

In the era of King Louis XIV (who lived from 1638–1715), France was the most powerful country in Europe. The kings of France had, for many generations, lived in great wealth and luxury. When Louis came to the throne, France was at the height of its power and glory. Louis, however, was not the best king France ever had. Instead of using his power to improve the lot of the poor people in his country, he surrounded himself with luxury and fine palaces. He considered himself to be the absolute owner of all things. As everything depends on the Sun for life, Louis believed that all of France depended on him – hence he demanded to be known as the Sun King.

Despite having a royal palace in Paris, he ordered another one built at Versailles, about 30km outside the city. Louis moved to Versailles, and forced all his nobles to do the same. He wanted them close at hand so that they would not *conspire* against him. The money for the *extravagant* life led by Louis and his nobles had to come from somewhere; it was raised by putting more and more taxes on the peasants of France, who as a result, became poorer and poorer and more and more dissatisfied with their condition.

Although France did have a Parliament at this time, Louis never allowed it to meet, preferring to make every decision himself. He had a team of ministers who ensured that his orders were carried out. Louis hated criticism and would not tolerate any opposition. People who disagreed with him were imprisoned without trial, usually in the Bastille, France's most famous prison.

While the king and his nobles lived in luxury in Versailles and in other palaces throughout the country, the people who dwelt in the cities and in the countryside often did not have enough to live on. During the reign of Louis, several revolts broke out in Paris, attempting to overthrow the king and reduce the burden of taxation. All these revolts were quickly and ruthlessly *suppressed* by Louis' loyal troops.

Louis' reign lasted for more than 50 years, during which the power and wealth of France declined considerably. The desire for new conquests encouraged him to make war against Spain, Holland and Germany. Each of these wars, however, ended in defeat for France and gradually, the power of France began to decline.

Also at this time, many people in France became Protestant. Louis would not allow them to practise their religion in peace and he enacted laws which persecuted them. 50,000 of these people, who were called Huguenots, were forced to flee abroad. Most of these were hard-working craftsmen who had made a big contribution to France's growth. They were very much missed after their departure.

Louis XIV died in 1715, still surrounded by luxury, though France itself was financially ruined from his wars and building programmes. The seeds of the French Revolution of 1789, when the peasants rebelled and killed their king and many nobles, were certainly sown during the reign of this *despotic* king.

Activities

A Answer these questions.

1. What age was Louis XIV when he died?
2. Did he improve the lot of poor people in France?
3. Why did he ask to be called the Sun King?
4. Where is Versailles situated?
5. Why did Louis want his nobles close at hand?
6. What happened to those who disagreed with him?
7. Why did revolts break out?
8. On his death, why was France financially ruined?
9. Who were the "Huguenots?"
10. Who later rebelled during the French Revolution?

B Write the words in *italics* in interesting sentences of your own.
Look up the words in your dictionary if you're unsure of their meaning.

C Summarise the story in your own words and in about ten sentences.

D Wordsearch: European Union Countries.
Unscramble the words and find them in the grid.

1. arfnce _____
2. prcysu _____
3. setnoai _____
4. inlfadn _____
5. ivltaa _____
6. aaltm _____
7. opaldn _____
8. olsavika _____
9. iensvloa _____
10. erianld _____
11. endswe _____
12. aghnuyr _____

w	x	p	a	h	f	y	r	a	g	n	u	h
p	r	l	f	h	i	c	e	k	k	h	n	g
p	c	u	a	i	n	o	t	s	e	d	k	y
x	d	m	f	r	l	c	e	d	y	p	p	c
z	n	d	g	e	a	g	p	x	v	d	y	s
t	a	d	z	l	n	k	d	z	c	p	x	l
d	l	c	m	a	d	k	m	a	r	r	p	o
b	o	x	s	n	p	l	n	u	t	i	l	v
c	p	p	v	d	p	m	s	l	p	n	o	a
e	c	n	a	r	f	a	i	v	t	a	l	k
a	i	n	e	v	o	l	s	v	e	a	n	i
y	n	d	g	d	n	t	d	y	y	x	w	a
y	m	b	k	m	b	a	n	e	d	e	w	s

E Can you write out the other 15 European Union Countries?

Cloze

A Write the passage using the words.

> hat sign century sneeze very believe many especially
> customary health Tuesday see health

Sneezing

People long ago believed that a sneeze – 'a little explosion in the head' – was a _____ from the gods which could foretell either good or evil fortune. The present custom of wishing the sneezer good _____ or fortune – to forestall possible bad luck – dates back at least to the Ancient Greeks. In the 17th _____ it was very impolite to omit the wish, and it was _____ to raise the _____ and bow at the same time.

Sneezing to the right denoted good fortune, _____ at the start of a journey; but to _____ to the left, or near a grave, was _____ unlucky. Sneezing three times before breakfast is thought to predict a present before the end of the week. Some people _____ it is a sign of good _____ to sneeze after a meal; anyone who does so regularly after dinner is expected to live to a great age.

There are _____ rhymes connected with sneezing. One runs: Monday for danger, _____ kiss a stranger, Wednesday for a letter, Thursday something better, Friday for sorrow, Saturday, _____ your lover tomorrow.

B Write the missing words.

> oceans contain invisible Antarctic least various heat
> evaporated leave prove rivers millions

Why is sea water salty?

Scientists believe that when the _____ were first formed _____ of years ago the sea water was fresh. As rivers pass over the land on their way to the sea, they wash out of the ground _____ kinds of salts. Sometimes we talk about freshwater _____ . No river is absolutely fresh. All rivers _____ a small percentage of salt which is being carried down to the sea. The _____ of the Sun evaporates water from the sea; that is, it turns the water into a kind of _____ vapour. When sea water is _____ , the salts in it are left behind.

You can _____ this yourself by boiling salt water in a pan. The water will all disappear as steam and _____ the salt at the bottom of the pan. The surface of the sea is generally more salty than it is lower down. In the Arctic and the _____ , where there are no great rivers to carry salts to the sea, the ocean is the _____ salty. The waters of the Dead Sea contain six times as much salt as the open ocean.

Grammar

> An **adjective** is a word that describes a noun or a pronoun. It may go before or after the noun or pronoun.
> Example: It is a **cloudy** and **cold** day.
> The day is **cloudy** and **cold**.

 A Write the sentences, choosing suitable adjectives.

> black   yellow   brown   evergreen   grey   hazel   red   white
> tawny   purple   friendly   fair-haired   blue   piebald

1. The gardener sprayed the _____ roses.
2. The _____ leaves withered and died.
3. The _____ horse jumped over the fence.
4. The elephant has _____ ivory tusks.
5. The _____ daffodils waved in the evening breeze.
6. The _____ beetle crawled under a mossy rock.
7. The bog was covered with clumps of _____ heather.
8. The _____ firs covered the mountainside.
9. The Vikings were _____ warriors.
10. The _____ owl hooted in the pine forest.
11. The squirrel cracked the _____ nuts.
12. The _____ dolphins swarmed around the boat.
13. A _____ mist hung over the valley.
14. The lark sang in the clear _____ sky.

 B Write the following groups of words in interesting sentences.
Example: chestnut, galloped, colt,
The **chestnut colt galloped** across the open plain.

1. timid, scurried, rabbit
2. little, hopped, robin
3. loathsome, glided, snake
4. tawny, flitted, owl
5. clammy, leaped, frog
6. faithful, barked, dog
7. saucy, screeched, parrot
8. ponderous, ambled, elephant
9. graceful, glided, swan
10. dainty, fluttered, butterfly
11. gentle, soared, lark
12. fallow, bounded, deer
13. gentle, frisked, lamb
14. hairy, swung, gorilla
15. plump, strutted, turkey
16. slimy, crawled, snail
17. speckled, darted, trout
18. grey, scampered, squirrel

C Rewrite the sentences using more descriptive phrases to replace the phrases in *italics*.

1. It was a *nice day*.
2. It was a *fabulous show*.
3. She is a *lovely person*.
4. I like *sweet things*.
5. They are *nice people*.
6. Sanjay had a *marvellous time*.
7. The dress had *pretty colours*.
8. It was a *very good game*.
9. The *bad* witch was *very cruel*.
10. The *brave* hunter tracked the *big animal*.

Writing

> A proofreader checks that a piece of writing is correct and ready for printing. Proofreaders check for correct spelling and punctuation.

 Proofread these sentences.
Each sentence has three mistakes in spelling or punctuation, or both.
Find the mistakes and then rewrite each sentence correctly.

1. "Oh no, she said. " i forgot my pensil case."
2. Where wood you like too go on holiday.
3. Ben dosen't no what he wants to do when he grows up
4. At the sweet shop I bought some chews a packet of crisps an ice lolly and a choclate bar.
5. We mite find out soon weather there was ever life on mars.
6. On saturday we're going to watch the football. do you want to come with us.
7. Ive got a new mobile phone and its amazing
8. Our school team won the cricket tornament, and I was very proud when they went to recieve the trophey.
9. Despite the constant rain forgetting the sleeping bags getting lost in the woods and the car breaking down the camping trip went really well.
10. "Do you enjoy english lessons he asked.

 Proofread this 'zany' weather forecast. Rewrite the article correctly.

No fare whether ahead this weakend folks. i'm afraid it's batten down the haches time as a storm of cats, dogs and elefants will strike on friday night. trees, houses even dinosores will be upruted by the gail force winds. So sleep tite and don't let the bed bugs bight.
What are you doing on saturday if you're going to the consert, then you'd better bring an ancor and chain it to your fut. their will be showers of hale sweeping across the country. some of the hailstones may bee as big, as bowling bawls.

Those of you driveing on the rodes should bring yours ise skates in case the car brakes down.

On sunday, there will be heavy falls of snoe. i guess yule all be making snowmans in your bakyards. do you fancy yourselph as a dare-devil. Why not go for a swim in the sub-zero see. it won't kil you, i think. So go on, have a grate weekend folks and enjoy this bewtiful weather. see you monday with more gud news.

Language

A

Descriptive words.
Group the following words under their correct headings.

cross	lonesome	frightened	jolly	sorrowful	delighted	scared	cheerful
annoyed	miserable	furious	joyful	terrified	gloomy	vexed	apprehensive

	Fear	Happiness	Anger	Sadness
1.	_____	_____	_____	_____
2.	_____	_____	_____	_____
3.	_____	_____	_____	_____
4.	_____	_____	_____	_____

B

Choose a suitable word from the given list to complete the phrase.
Write each phrase in a sentence.

tribe	river	shoe	clock	chair	bottle	saw	needle	hill	corn

1. the leg of a _____
2. the brow of a _____
3. the tongue of a _____
4. the mouth of a _____
5. the neck of a _____
6. the teeth of a _____
7. the eye of a _____
8. the face of a _____
9. the head of a _____
10. the ear of _____

C

Places.

vineyard	aviary	court	gallery	hold	nursery	zoo
	theatre	hospital	mint			

1. A ship's cargo is kept in a _____ .
2. Plays are performed in a _____ .
3. Young shrubs are grown in a _____ .
4. Paintings are kept in a _____ .
5. Wild animals are kept in a _____ .
6. Birds are kept in an _____ .
7. Tennis is played on a _____ .
8. Money is made in a _____ .
9. Operations are performed in a _____ .
10. Grapes are grown in a _____ .

45

Read the story.

Earthquakes

An earthquake is a shaking of the ground caused by the sudden breaking and shifting of large sections of the Earth's rocky outer shell. This process is happening all the time. Scientists estimate that there are more than 8,000 *minor* earthquakes each day. Of these, only about 1,000 are strong enough to be felt. At least 40 moderate earthquakes cause damage somewhere in the world each year. A really powerful earthquake only occurs, on average, once every two years, but when it does, the results can be devastating.

Most earthquakes occur along a fault – a *fracture* where sections of rock repeatedly slide past each other. Stresses in the Earth cause large blocks of rock along a fault to strain, or bend. When the stress on the rock becomes great enough, the rock breaks and snaps into a new position, causing the shaking of an earthquake. About eighty per cent of the world's major earthquakes occur in an area called the Ring of Fire, around the edge of the Pacific Ocean.

An earthquake causes damage in many different ways. During a very powerful earthquake the ground on either side of a fault may suddenly open up. Any structure that spans the fault may be torn apart, rock and soil along a slope may be loosened, triggering a landslide, or the banks of rivers and lakes may be torn apart, causing flooding. An earthquake on the ocean floor can create one or more large, *destructive* waves called tsunamis. Tsunamis may build to heights of more than thirty metres when they reach shallow water near shore. Ground shaking causes structures to move violently. Buildings may slide off their foundations, collapse, or be shaken apart. Fires may start if a quake *ruptures* gas or power lines. Sewage lines may break, and sewage may seep into water supplies. Drinking contaminated water can cause serious diseases.

In areas where earthquakes are likely, knowing where to build and how to build can help reduce the effects of a quake. Buildings should not be built on areas near faults, on flood plains or on steep slopes that may be *subject* to landslides. Smaller buildings are bolted to their foundations and have special supports called "shear walls", which help resist rocking forces. Medium-sized buildings are often protected with devices called base isolators, which act like shock absorbers between the building and its foundation. Skyscrapers must be anchored deeply into the ground and need a specially strengthened framework. In earthquake prone areas, heavy appliances and furniture are often fastened down to prevent them from falling over when the building shakes.

Activities

 A   **Answer these questions.**

1. How many earthquakes are there each day around the world?
2. How frequently do very powerful earthquakes occur?
3. What is a fault?
4. What is the "Ring of Fire"?
5. Why are there sometimes fires after an earthquake?
6. Describe three other effects of earthquakes.
7. In earthquake-prone areas, where should people avoid putting buildings?
8. How are smaller buildings often protected from earthquakes?
9. What are base isolators?
10. Name one way that skyscrapers can be made earthquake-proof.

Epicentre —
Fault line —
Focus —

B   **Write the words in *italics* in interesting sentences of your own.**
Look up the words in your dictionary if you're unsure of their meaning.

C   **Copy the paragraph and replace then with some of the words from the box.**

> at   midday   shortly   afterwards   suddenly   eventually   soon
> while   unfortunately   almost   immediately   straight   away

Caius came to collect the boys from school. (*Then*) they wandered back home through the bustling street. (*Then*) Marcus began kicking a stone along the ruts worn away by the carts that trundled along the roads after sunset. (*Then*) they reached the crossroads. Caius stopped to chat with friends who collect water at the fountain. (*Then*) they waited, Marcus and Julius peered into the shops. (*Then*) the shopkeepers were beginning to prepare for the midday rest. (*Then*) they closed the great wooden shutters. Caius crossed the street and (*then*) Marcus and Julius followed him home.

 D   **Wordsearch: The Earth.**
Find the words in the grid.

1. volcano
2. rock
3. forest
4. ocean
5. mountain
6. globe
7. atmosphere
8. oxygen
9. temperature
10. island
11. continent
12. pollution

p	e	r	u	t	a	r	e	p	m	e	t	g
t	a	b	l	o	y	y	g	d	a	a	l	k
n	o	n	a	c	l	o	v	n	e	o	m	o
o	k	l	o	b	x	c	p	p	b	x	y	g
i	s	l	a	n	d	e	o	e	v	o	l	p
t	x	s	u	d	d	a	x	h	e	c	c	k
u	x	f	l	r	k	n	n	d	e	p	d	t
l	p	p	e	n	i	a	t	n	u	o	m	s
l	d	x	k	r	n	n	o	s	t	m	k	e
o	c	c	o	n	t	i	n	e	n	t	x	r
p	z	c	t	p	n	n	e	g	y	x	o	o
m	k	o	d	p	h	h	y	z	k	n	o	f
m	z	a	t	m	o	s	p	h	e	r	e	g

Cloze

A Write the passage using the words.

seems	size	weigh	object	nothing	times	black	flabbergasted
under	dimmer	heavy	galaxy	spin			

Black holes

Scientists were _____ when they discovered that there are black holes in space. How could they explain them? It _____ that some stars are so massive that they begin to collapse _____ their own weight. As the star crushes itself, it gets dimmer and _____ and its material becomes very dense and very _____ . A star that condenses itself down to about the _____ of the Earth is known as a White Dwarf. A teaspoon of material from it would _____ about five tons!

But some stars collapse completely into _____ : a black hole is left. It is believed that these holes _____ round at the incredible speed of 1,000 _____ per second. Any _____ that fell into a black hole would be torn into a billion parts. Our _____ may contain millions of these amazing _____ holes.

B Write the missing words.

times	victims	native	coils	crushing	snake's	between	everything
break	stomach	sticking	usually	body	swallow	feathers	swell

Boa constrictor

The boa constrictor is a _____ of South and Central America. It dines on birds, lizards and mammals. Having seized its prey with its backward-pointed teeth, the snake _____ its strong muscular _____ around the victim. The terrific pressure applied causes the animal to suffocate and die of heart failure. Since the _____ teeth are unsuitable for _____ and chewing food, _____ eaten must be swallowed whole. The amazing reptile can _____ out its elastic jaws to surround and _____ a creature many _____ its own size. The skin _____ the scales stretches out to store the food. Powerful digestive juices in the snake's _____ help dissolve and _____ up the big meal. The snake _____ swallows its _____ head first. This prevents the fur or _____ of the unfortunate victim from _____ in the snake's throat.

Grammar

Adjectives formed from proper nouns begin with capital letters.
Example: The **Spanish** footballer married the **Mexican** dancer.

A **Write the sentences, inserting the adjectives.**

1. The shopkeeper bought a chest of _____ tea. (*India*)
2. My aunt has a _____ cat and a _____ sheepdog. (*Siam, Scotland*)
3. I enjoy _____ movies and _____ operas. (*America, Italy*)
4. The _____ restaurant serves _____ cheese and _____ wines. (*China, Denmark, France*)
5. The _____ Government expelled the _____ diplomat. (*Russia, Britain*)
6. We flew over the _____ mountains and the _____ Sea. (*Wales, Ireland*)
7. The lady bought an expensive _____ perfume. (*Paris*)
8. Switzerland is famous for its _____ rescue climbers. (*Alps*)

B **Form adjectives from the nouns. Use your dictionary if you are unsure.**

1. adventure _____	11. deceit _____	21. music _____
2. affection _____	12. disorder _____	22. misery _____
3. angel _____	13. energy _____	23. mountain _____
4. anger _____	14. explore _____	24. nation _____
5. anxiety _____	15. fire _____	25. picture _____
6. attraction _____	16. fury _____	26. sorrow _____
7. child _____	17. giant _____	27. success _____
8. caution _____	18. hero _____	28. terror _____
9. coward _____	19. joy _____	29. value _____
10. comfort _____	20. merriment _____	30. wool _____

C **Write the sentences with adjectives formed from the nouns.**

1. The _____ lady helped the poor. (*influenced*)
2. The _____ occasion was marred by heavy rain. (*joy*)
3. The old beggar was a _____ sight to behold. (*pity*)
4. The _____ warrior brandished his sword. (*danger*)
5. We were outnumbered and the situation was _____ . (*hope*)
6. The _____ man dived into the river and saved the girl. (*courage*)
7. She is a _____ lady. (*charity*)
8. The actress lived in a _____ apartment. (*luxury*)
9. The _____ child went to bed. (*obey*)
10. The _____ team paraded around the town. (*victory*)

Writing

A Look at the map. You are an explorer who has just discovered Lake Wara Wara. You have come from point **A**. Write an account of what happened. Write it as a diary if you wish. (Remember not to over-use **and**, **but** or **then**.)

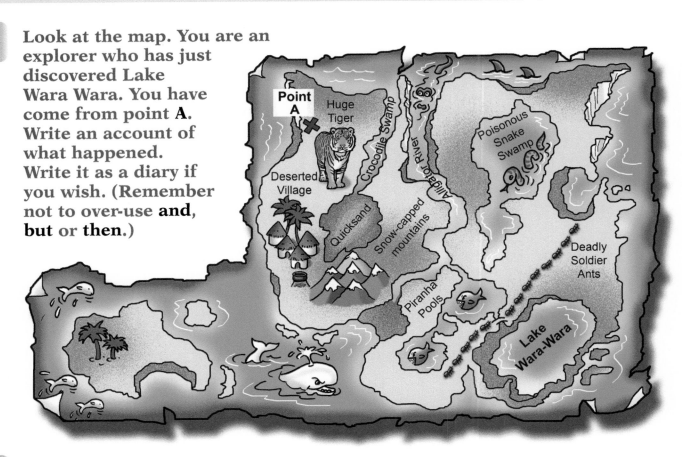

B You and your friend went on a jungle adventure. Write an account, in diary form if you wish. You might like to use some of these ideas and vocabulary.

hardy pack-animals	the prowling jaguar
hot and humid (damp)	king of the jungle
tangled vegetation	trudged onwards
hacked away furiously	encountered huge tiger
dense canopy of foliage (leaves)	terrified and trembling
dark and sinister	mortal danger
swarming flies	kept upwind
teeming beetles	crept away slowly
gloriously coloured butterflies	advanced steadily
chattering monkeys	an immense river
whistling and screeching	Amazon
twittering and chirping of birds	paddled canoes
majestic eagle soaring	swift current
deep into the rainforest	dangerous rapids
treacherous quicksand	gigantic snakes
escaped unscathed (without injury)	

Language

 A Write two words for each of these suffixes.

able	like	ant	ion	hood	fy
acy	er	fold	ed	less	ment
en	ate	ess	ful	ee	ish
ly	ive	dom	ible	ician	wise
ary	ous	form	ation	ism	ways

 B Write the sentences, completing the words with a suitable suffix.

1. The prisoner of war tunnelled his way to free_____ .
2. In order to start the machine you must push the lever in a clock_____ direction.
3. Martin Luther was the founding father of protestant_____ .
4. The home_____ man was given shelter for the night.
5. She was a very hard-working and efficient manager_____ .
6. He rang the office to in_____ his employer that he was ill.
7. She sat down in a comfort_____ armchair and read the newspaper.
8. The mission_____ devoted his life to working for the poor.
9. They listened attentively as the story began to un_____ .
10. A cure for the ill_____ has been discovered late_____ .

 C Write the sentences, finding a word to match the suffix.

1. She earned a _____hood as a solicitor.
2. There will be many _____ful candidates in the next election.
3. The _____less gambler lost a fortune in Las Vegas.
4. Our babysitter is a very _____able person.
5. The pupil was given extra homework because of his _____ish behaviour.
6. The _____ive model wore a beautiful evening dress.
7. The musician played a _____ly jig on the violin.
8. The orchestra played the first _____ment of the symphony.
9. The motorist was heavily fined for _____ous driving.
10. The brave _____ion of the fireman saved many lives.

Reading

A Read the story.

Elephants

Elephants are the largest animals that live on land. There are two main types of elephant: African elephants, which have large ears, and Indian elephants, which have smaller ears and are slightly shorter. African elephants live only in Africa, south of the Sahara Desert, while Indian elephants live in parts of India and Southeast Asia.

Because elephants are both extremely strong and highly *intelligent*, people have been taming and training them for thousands of years. Nearly two and a half thousand years ago Alexander the Great defeated a Persian army that rode elephants. Just over a hundred years later, Hannibal of Carthage used elephants to cross the Alps and invade Italy.

During the nineteenth century, an African elephant named Jumbo was the *prime* attraction at London Zoo. Visitors came from all over the world to see Jumbo, who was the largest animal in *captivity* at that time, standing 3.4 metres tall and weighing more than 6,600 kilograms. Jumbo was so famous that the word "jumbo" began to be used to describe anything extremely large.

Today, working elephants are still used to carry heavy loads in some Asian countries, and people throughout the world enjoy watching elephants in zoos. In Africa and parts of Asia it is still possible to see wild elephants in their natural environment, but how much longer this will be possible is uncertain, as the number of wild elephants has been *declining* steadily.

One reason for the decrease in the wild elephant *population* is hunting. Throughout history, people have hunted elephants for their ivory tusks. Until about twenty years ago, tens of thousands of elephants, especially African elephants, were killed every year. Ivory is used to make jewellery, carvings, piano keys and Japanese "signature seals" – traditional carved stamps used to print a person's name. In the last twenty years, laws designed to protect elephants have been passed in many of the countries where they live, making it illegal to hunt them.

Another cause of the decline in elephant numbers is more difficult to deal with. As the human population increases, more and more of the land where elephants used to live is being used by humans. Every year, farming and industry destroy more and more of the elephants' natural habitat. Despite the efforts of many conservation groups to save the elephant, it is not certain that there will be any wild elephants left in fifty years' time.

Activities

A Answer these questions.

1. What are the two main types of elephant?
2. How can you tell them apart?
3. Where do Indian elephants live?
4. What characteristics of the elephant make it useful to humans?
5. Describe one way in which humans used elephants in ancient times.
6. Describe one way in which humans use elephants today.
7. Why were elephants hunted?
8. Explain the origin of the word "jumbo".
9. Why has the number of wild elephants decreased?
10. Why will the number of wild elephants probably carry on decreasing?

B Look up the words in *italics* in your dictionary.
Write a sentence for each one.

C Summarise the story in your own words.
Use about ten sentences.

D Wordsearch: Sea Animals.
Unscramble the words and find them in the grid.

1. skahr _____
2. dinolph _____
3. ewahl _____
4. poserpoi _____
5. sidqu _____
6. fatishc _____
7. eljlishyf _____
8. sharfist _____
9. yra _____
10. teoysr _____
11. ele _____
12. topocus _____

o	w	s	h	a	r	k	e	e	c
r	c	t	y	d	u	i	s	o	a
p	a	t	i	o	s	i	h	d	t
f	g	u	o	l	o	h	s	j	f
k	q	l	z	p	x	c	i	v	i
s	b	n	r	h	u	m	f	q	s
w	r	o	e	i	r	s	r	t	h
y	p	a	u	n	w	h	a	l	e
e	e	l	y	o	y	s	t	e	r
j	e	l	l	y	f	i	s	h	i

Writing

> **Interjections** are words 'thrown' into a sentence to express some sudden emotion or feeling, such as joy, sorrow, pain, triumph or surprise. An exclamation mark (!) is written after an interjection. Examples: **Hush! Hurrah! Oh! Alas!**

 A Choose the most suitable interjections to fill the blank spaces.

> Stop!   Bravo!   Open up!   Alas!   Hello!   Oh!   Hush!   Good gracious!   Halt!
> Shame on you!   Help!   Ouch!   Hurrah!

1. _____ ! Who's speaking?
2. _____ ! Don't make a sound.
3. _____ ! That hurts.
4. _____ ! He died young.
5. _____ ! We have won the cup.
6. _____ ! What is that?
7. _____ ! You pinched me.

8. _____ ! Man overboard.
9. _____ ! Who goes there?
10. _____ ! He rescued the little girl.
11. _____ ! Police on duty.
12. _____ ! Road blocked.
13. _____ ! The little girl is crying.

Exclamations!
To exclaim means to cry out in anger, surprise, joy, sadness, pain, warning, and such exclamations should be followed by an exclamation mark.
Example: someone admiring a view might say: "What a marvellous sight this is!"
Note: an interjection need not necessarily be used with these exclamations.

B Write the exclamations which the following people might make.

1. A captain urging on his team.
2. A person warning a child to keep away from something.
3. An explorer on making a great discovery.
4. A person whose holiday has been spoiled by bad weather.
5. A player shouting to a team-mate on the football pitch.
6. A doctor warning a patient on the dangers of smoking.
7. A jockey speaking as he crosses the finishing line.
8. An angry policeman telling off a careless motorist.

C Questions and Riddles. Always begin a question with a capital letter and end it with a question mark. Write out these riddles correctly.

1. What gets wetter the more it dries.
2. What gets bigger the more you take from it.
3. Which is heavier: a kilogram of stones or a kilogram of feathers.
4. What is made dirty by washing.
5. What is black and white and red all over.
6. What goes up and never comes down.
7. Where does a fish keep its money.
8. Where did the zebra cross the road.

Grammar

> **Adjectives** change their form when they are used to compare one thing with another.
> Example:
> Laura is **tall**. Ben is **taller**. Ahmed is the **tallest**.
> **tall** – the **positive** degree of the adjective.
> **taller** – the **comparative** degree of the adjective.
> **tallest** – the **superlative** degree of the adjective.

A Copy and complete the table.

Positive	Comparative	Superlative
1. young	younger	youngest
2. red	_____	_____
3. bright	_____	_____
4. noble	_____	_____
5. empty	_____	_____
6. pretty	_____	_____
7. lucky	_____	_____
8. generous	more generous	most generous
9. cautious	_____	_____
10. brilliant	_____	_____

B Be careful. These adjectives are irregular. Complete the table.

1. good	better	best
2. bad	_____	_____
3. little	_____	_____
4. much	_____	_____
5. old	_____	_____
6. late	_____	_____
7. up	upper	uppermost
8. far	_____	_____

C Write the sentences, choosing the correct words.

1. This boy made the _____ number of errors. (*fewest*, *least*)
2. Hari was _____ than his brother. (*more cautious*, *most cautious*)
3. The carpenter sawed off the _____ end of the log. (*rougher*, *roughest*)
4. There were _____ spectators than runners at the sports stadium. (*less*, *fewer*)
5. He is the _____ boy in the choir. (*smaller*, *smallest*)
6. The _____ team won the rugby final. (*best*, *better*)
7. Hana is the _____ of the two girls. (*taller*, *tallest*)
8. My _____ sister is in hospital. (*oldest*, *old*)

Writing

Write two list poems. One about trees and one about leaves.

Example:

Happiness
Happiness is Friday.
Happiness is summer.
Happiness is French fries.
Happiness is no homework.
Happiness is staying up late.
Happiness is me!

Trees	Leaves
Trees are friendly	Leaves are waving
Trees are _____ .	Leaves are whispering
Trees are _____ .	Leaves are _____ .
Trees are _____ .	Leaves are _____ .
Trees are _____ .	Leaves are _____ .
Trees are _____ .	Leaves are _____ .
Trees are _____ .	Leaves are _____ .
Trees are _____ .	Leaves are _____ .

B In an acrostic poem the title of the poem is spelled by using the first letter of each line. Look at this acrostic poem called *Giants*. Write your own acrostic poem about giants.

Gently up the lane
In boots as big as trees
A friendless giant came
No others did he see
The town is always empty
So frightening is he.

C Now choose two titles from the list and do the same as above.

Ghosts   Dragon   Unicorn   Fairy   Troll

D Illustrate your poems.

56

Language

 A Which is the odd one out in the following lists.

1. seal, sheep, skunk, sparrow, squirrel
2. pike, trout, whale, herring, cod
3. rabbit, badger, otter, fox, hare
4. peach, pineapple, pear, potato, plum
5. oyster, mussel, octopus, periwinkle, whelk
6. fir tree, yew tree, pine tree, beech tree
7. donkey, kangaroo, mule, horse
8. magpie, penguin, cuckoo, robin, blackbird
9. stallion, filly, colt, buffalo, foal

B In the following, give one word meaning the **same** as and one the **opposite** of.

Word	Same	Opposite
rich	wealthy	poor
kind	_____	_____
fat	_____	_____
bitter	_____	_____
meek	_____	_____
round	_____	_____
end	_____	_____
hard	_____	_____
courageous	_____	_____
permit	_____	_____

C A compound word is made up of two or more separate words.
Example: ash + tray = ashtray.
Complete the following words in order to form compound words.

1. _____board
2. _____man
3. _____post
4. _____case
5. _____cup
6. _____keeper

7. _____father
8. _____port
9. _____ball
10. _____mine
11. _____cloth
12. _____wreck

D Use these similes to make interesting sentences.

1. As quick as lightning.
2. As clean as a new pin.
3. As clear as crystal.
4. As silent as the grave.
5. As busy as an ant.
6. As soft as putty.
7. As fast as a hare.

8. As black as coal.
9. As heavy as lead.
10. As fresh as a daisy.
11. As swift as a deer.
12. As graceful as a swan.
13. As poor as a church mouse.
14. As weak as water.

Reading

A Read the story.

The Bears

Suddenly, Ned felt that he must look over his shoulder. Whether it was that he noticed the bear looking at something *beyond* him, or that he heard sounds behind him, he was not sure; but he simply had to look round. If a man's hair can stand on end with horror, then Ned Blake's hair stood on end. He was sick with fear; so shaken that he nearly fell off the ledge. For there at the far end, blocking his way, stood another huge grizzly bear.

Ned was so dazed with terror that at first he thought he was going mad and seeing grizzlies everywhere. Yet the two bears were real; and one thing soon became plain – he was trapped.

Desperately he looked down into the *ravine*. He would certainly fall and be *dashed* to pieces if he attempted that route. He looked up at the rock wall above him. It was so *sheer* that not even a monkey could have managed to scale it.

Bitter thoughts rose in the man's mind as he remembered his rifle lying in the *gorge* below. A *menacing* growl from each side answered him. Ned lost his cool completely, and screamed and screamed again.

The next few seconds remained in Ned Blake's memory ever afterwards as a confused nightmare, ended mercifully by the touch of a *dangling* rope on his shoulder. Pulling himself together he grasped the rope firmly, and heaved himself up until he was half-way up the rockwall and could pause, feet *braced* against the rock, and looking down on the bears. Their growls became louder and angrier. Ned, not knowing that the animals were more interested in each other than in him, was *faint* with fear. When his brother finally dragged him to safety, he had only strength enough left to stagger away from the edge and gasp, "Let's go home."

The two bears advanced towards each other step by step – in no hurry, yet perfectly ready to fight.

Activities

A Answer these questions.

1. What was it that terrified Ned so much?
2. Pick out three phrases which show how frightened he was.
3. Two reasons why "he simply had to look round" are suggested in paragraph one. What are they?
4. "He thought he was going mad." Why?
5. "He was trapped." Explain in what way he was trapped.
6. "The animals were more interested in each other than in him." What does this mean?
7. Who lowered the rope to Ned?
8. Write another title for the story.
9. Did the two bears move quickly or slowly towards each other?
10. How did Ned look back on this event in later life?

B Look up the words in *italics* in your dictionary. Write a sentence for each one.

C Summarise the story in your own words. Use about ten sentences.

D Write the group phrases and find the group words in the grid. Use your dictionary if unsure.

brood	nest	plague	school	troop	herd	gaggle	flock	shoal
building	skulk	sloth	litter	team	string			

1. A _____ of bears
2. A _____ of chickens
3. A _____ of birds
4. A _____ of geese
5. A _____ of elephants
6. A _____ of rabbits
7. A _____ of insects
8. A _____ of whales
9. A _____ of herring
10. A _____ of monkeys
11. A _____ of foxes
12. A _____ of oxen
13. A _____ of puppies
14. A _____ of rooks
15. A _____ of horses

k	r	h	h	x	t	e	a	m	d	d	b	p
k	d	e	h	a	l	y	y	p	e	h	u	u
m	r	p	g	a	g	g	l	e	u	i	i	d
d	g	d	a	e	p	p	d	l	g	d	l	k
b	b	x	i	r	d	i	n	g	a	k	d	m
k	b	o	b	r	o	o	d	u	l	k	i	g
m	d	r	g	m	p	d	k	b	p	c	n	g
m	o	k	k	l	u	k	s	b	y	o	g	n
n	c	m	p	s	n	t	h	d	y	l	g	i
s	h	o	a	l	t	r	o	o	p	f	h	r
s	h	p	d	o	s	h	p	x	g	g	p	t
z	n	p	l	t	e	l	i	t	t	e	r	s
w	n	d	h	h	n	s	c	h	o	o	l	s

Cloze

A

Write the passage using the words.

fact	multiplied	parent	extinct	factor	Dutch
weight	put	now	flightless	soon	Indian	was

Dodo

The Dodo is an _____ bird. They were giant birds
weighing 25kg or more, at least seven times the
_____ of any pigeon which can fly. They were
_____ birds, that lived on Mauritius Island,
in the _____ Ocean. The island _____
discovered in 1507 by the Portuguese. _____,
French and English ships _____ stopped there.
Sailors used to kill the Dodos for food. Another
_____ which led to the rapid extinction of the
Dodo was the _____ that pigs and monkeys
_____ ashore by the Portuguese _____ rapidly,
the monkeys ate the Dodo eggs, and the pigs killed off
the _____ birds. The fact that the Dodo was a flightless bird
was an obvious disadvantage. The bird survived until 1681, and is
_____ extinct.

B

Write the passage using the words.

anniversary	committee	Sweden	first	awards	publicly	established
prizes	secret	decide	each	won	found	only	contribution
	invented	annual	recommend			

Alfred Nobel, the scientist from _____ who _____
dynamite, bequeathed most of his huge fortune to _____ the
Nobel Prizes when he died in 1896. A fund was _____ for five
_____ awards to those who had made the biggest _____ in
physics, chemistry, medicine, literature and peace. The prizes
were _____ awarded in 1901. Five committees sit in _____
to _____ the prize-winners. Except for the peace prize, which
can be _____ by a group, _____ can be given _____ to
individuals. The peace prize is _____ awarded in Oslo on
10 December _____ year, the _____ of Nobel's death. The
other four _____ are awarded in Stockholm. If you were on
the peace _____ or the literature committee, who would you
_____ for the Nobel Prize?

60

Grammar

> Most **verbs** are **action** or **doing** words. A verb can be one word, two words or even three words.
> Examples: The cat **chased** the mouse.
> The girl **was trying** her best.

A Write the sentences with the most suitable verbs.

1. The hungry hawks (*swallowed*, *devoured*, *smothered*) the dead sparrow.
2. The old couple (*strode*, *moved*, *strolled*) along the beach.
3. The upset customer (*argued*, *complained*, *grumbled*) to the manager.
4. The timid rabbit (*scampered*, *charged*, *flitted*) across the meadow.
5. The brave soldiers (*fought*, *defended*, *opposed*) their fortress.
6. The goat (*bit*, *ate*, *chewed*) my hat.
7. The police car (*bounded*, *screeched*, *glided*) to a halt.
8. Clear crystal water (*gushed*, *pumped*, *gulped*) from the rock.
9. Forked lightning (*struck*, *smashed*, *cracked*) the clock tower in the village.
10. The injured athlete (*gripped*, *groaned*) with pain.

B Write the sentences choosing your own verbs.

1. The bus _____ on the icy road.
2. The jet aircraft _____ across the sky.
3. The nervous soldier _____ through the jungle.
4. The audience greatly _____ the concert.
5. The old steam engine _____ along the track.
6. The agile dancer _____ through the air.
7. The volcano _____ during the night.
8. A thick blanket of snow _____ the gardens.
9. The startled deer _____ through the long grass.

C Write this passage in the future tense.

Juan raced home from school. He ate his dinner and then went to the Post Office to withdraw some money from his Savings Account. Once he had some cash, he headed for the Shopping Centre. At the Shopping Centre he looked for the Sports Shop. It was situated at the very end of the arcade and as he entered he immediately noticed the boxes of football boots on the shelves. It took him about fifteen minutes to choose a suitable pair. He hoped they would help him win the final next week.

Writing

A   Complete the following story.

Stealthily we tiptoed down the narrow winding staircase. The haunting silence of the castle sent cold shivers down my spine. Just as we were about to return Femi cried out, "Look! a rusty door."

B   Complete the following story.

The old fortune-teller sat there in silence. She had enormous golden rings dangling from her ears. I was feeling nervous as I sat down. In a soft whisper she murmured, "…

C   Complete the following story.

Foolishly I had taken my uncle's boat without his permission. I had scarcely reached the middle of the river when the fast ebbing tide gripped the boat. Too late I realised my danger.

Language

A Change these nouns into verbs.

argument _____	apology _____	success _____
laughter _____	confusion _____	memory _____
generator _____	hesitation _____	entrance _____
failure _____	complaint _____	discussion _____

B Write the names of the class in alphabetical order.

S. Turner	B. Butcher	R. Summers
R. Connolly	A. Patel	R. Burns
J. Brown	J. Jones	P. Anderson
C. Burton	B. Summer	R. Celini
B. Pasternak	P. McKenna	B. Whelan
C. Parker	J. Ryan	K. Johnson

C These three words do not change if spelt backwards: **eye**; **eve**; **noon**. Can you find twelve others?

1. _____
2. _____
3. _____
4. _____
5. _____
6. _____

7. _____
8. _____
9. _____
10. _____
11. _____
12. _____

D Write **they're**, **their** or **there** in the blank spaces below.

_____ wasn't a cloud in the sky. The children put _____ coats on, as it was freezing outside. _____ mother waved goodbye to them and remarked, 'I wonder why _____ so chirpy today! I hope _____ careful'. When they reached the frozen lake, they stood _____ and gazed at it for a while, before starting to skate. Suddenly _____ was a loud crack. _____ was no time to lose. They skated furiously to the edge and when Barry lost a skate he just left it _____ on the ice. Then an enormous hole opened right before _____ very eyes. As they trudged wearily inside, _____ mother sighed, '_____ back already. They must have missed me!'

Reading

A Read the story.

Apollo 13

The Apollo 13 space mission, which blasted off on 11 April 1970, was due to make the third *lunar* landing. While on the Moon, the crew, James Lovell, Fred Haise and Jack Swigert, would collect rock samples, so scientists could learn more about the age and origin of the Earth's only natural *satellite*. The first two days of the flight went smoothly, but after fifty-six hours the crew heard a loud bang and felt a sudden jolt. Alarms started blaring and warning lights showed that one oxygen tank was empty, the other was losing pressure, and power was draining from the fuel cells that supplied the spacecraft with light, heat and electricity.

The "Lunar Module", the small craft designed to land on the Moon, was undamaged, so the astronauts switched off the power in the main spacecraft and moved into the Lunar Module. Mission Control instructed the crew to use the Lunar Module's engines to alter the course of the spacecraft. This course alteration pushed the craft into the influence of the Moon's gravity, which would then "slingshot" it back towards the Earth.

Although the Lunar Module had its own power and oxygen, it wasn't designed to support so many people for such a long time. The astronauts switched off everything that wasn't needed for life support, in the hope that power would last until they got back to Earth. Water was in short supply and the temperature fell close to freezing, making it very uncomfortable.

Before the spacecraft re-entered the Earth's atmosphere, the lunar module was *ejected*, and the crew moved back into the main part of the spacecraft. Would the spacecraft power back up, or would the remaining power have drained from the fuel cells? There was an added danger: the low temperatures had created condensation on the walls. This meant the electrical circuits could *short out* when the power was turned back on. To the astronauts' relief, the power came back safely.

Four days after the accident, the spacecraft splashed down in the Pacific Ocean. Despite grave danger, all three astronauts had returned home safely. It's hardly surprising, then, that the Apollo 13 mission is often referred to as a "successful failure."

Activities

A Answer these questions.

1. What was the purpose of the Apollo 13 mission?
2. How many missions had landed men on the Moon before Apollo 13?
3. When did the accident take place?
4. What problems did the accident cause?
5. Why did the astronauts have to move into the Lunar Module?
6. Why did the spacecraft have to change course after the accident?
7. Why didn't the astronauts switch on all of the Lunar Module's systems?
8. For how many days were the astronauts in danger?
9. What do you think people mean when they describe the Apollo 13 mission as a "successful failure"?
10. What caused the accident on Apollo 13? Use reference books or the Internet to find out.

B Look up the words in *italics* in your dictionary. Write a sentence for each one.

C Summarise the story in your own words. Use about ten sentences.

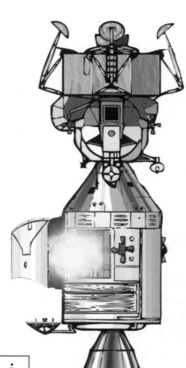

D Wordsearch: Apollo 13. Find the words in the grid.

1. astronaut
2. mission
3. Moon
4. apollo
5. spacecraft
6. rocket
7. accident
8. successful
9. lunar
10. failure

q	u	a	l	s	s	w	e	r	i
y	t	p	l	u	n	a	r	a	b
m	s	j	a	c	r	s	g	h	o
i	j	f	c	c	o	t	w	s	t
s	p	a	c	e	c	r	a	f	t
s	p	i	i	s	k	o	p	o	n
i	l	l	d	s	e	n	o	n	o
o	k	u	e	f	t	a	l	m	o
n	c	r	n	u	i	u	l	v	M
b	n	e	t	l	u	t	o	z	r

Cloze

A   Write the story using the words.

life	kidnapped	abolished	published	sea	trade	business
because	buy	officer	campaigning	across	adventure	

Olaudah Equiano (c.1745–1797)

Olaudah Equiano is famous for his autobiography, in which he told his remarkable _____ story, and for the work he undertook campaigning to abolish the slave _____ .

Olaudah grew up as the son of a chief in Guinea, but around the age of eleven he and his sister were _____ and sold into slavery. A few years later he was bought by Michael Pascal, a British naval _____ , who brought him to England, where he learned to read and write.

Although Equiano fought for the British navy for several years, he was cheated of his pay and was sold to another _____ captain who took him to the Caribbean and sold him to a merchant called Robert King.

Robert King treated his slaves extremely badly. Equiano, however, was luckier than most of the slaves on King's plantation. _____ he could read and write, he was given a responsible job and after three years he had saved enough money to _____ his freedom.

After becoming a free man, he returned to England and set up in _____ as a hairdresser, but he loved _____ and soon returned to sea.

In 1773, he joined a voyage of exploration to find a northwest passage to India _____ the North Pole and in 1775 he became involved in a project to set up a new plantation in Central America.

Equiano _____ his autobiography in the spring of 1789. He sold the book throughout Britain, undertaking lecture tours and actively _____ to abolish the slave trade.

The efforts of Equiano and the abolitionist movement were successful in the end, but it took nearly forty-five years before slavery was _____ in Britain.

Grammar

> **The Past Participle**
> (i) The **past tense** of a verb stands on its own.
>   Examples: You **came**. She **went**. We **sang**.
> (ii) The **past participle** requires another verb with it, some part of the verb 'to be' or 'to have'.
>   Examples: He **has come**. It **was taken**.

 A Complete this table.

Present Tense	Past Tense	Past Participle
They fly	_____	_____
We know	_____	_____
You steal	_____	_____
She rises	_____	_____
He creeps	_____	_____
I wear	_____	_____
They forget	_____	_____
You draw	_____	_____
We awake	_____	_____
They ring	_____	_____
He speaks	_____	_____

B Write the sentences, choosing the correct form of the verb.

1. They had (*come, came*) from miles around to attend the festival.
2. As soon as he had (*ate, eaten*) his meal he (*run, ran*) out the door.
3. We had (*swam, swum*) as far as the island in the river before he (*spoke, spoken*).
4. The sheriff (*known, knew*) that the horse had been (*stole, stolen*).
5. The boy had (*lay, lain*) there for hours.
6. If I had (*went, gone*) for the doctor in time the man would not have (*froze, frozen*) to death.
7. The old man (*knew, known*) that his daughter had (*win, won*) the prize.
8. When I had (*drawn, drew*) the sketch I (*gave, given*) it to the lady.
9. She (*written, wrote*) a letter to her friend but had (*forget, forgotten*) to post it.
10. The bicycle which he (*rode, ridden*) had been (*stole, stolen*).
11. The boy (*ran, run*) away after he had (*broke, broken*) the window.
12. No sooner had he (*rose, risen*) than a fat rabbit (*ran, run*) across the field.
13. He had scarcely (*awoke, awakened*) when it (*began, begun*) to snow.
14. The coat he (*chose, chosen*) to buy was (*tore, torn*).
15. The mayoress (*shaken, shook*) hands with the soprano who had (*sang, sung*) in the concert.

Writing

Opening sentences that give variety to your essay-writing.

In the distance …	Breathless we …
On reaching the …	Continuing …
Here the …	As we …
Dismounting, …	Occasionally …
After a short rest …	On approaching the …
It seemed …	Leaving the …
After some time …	Eventually …

 A Write a descriptive story about a cycling trip with your friends.

glorious afternoon   gentle breeze
fleecy white clouds   destination
peace and contentment
hum and drone of insects
wooded hillside   stately pines
grove of silver-grey birch
purple heather in bloom
rushing mountain stream
sparkling blue lake
ruins of an old castle
shrouded peak tops   pearly haze
natural trail   explored hidden paths
enjoyable afternoon
the return journey

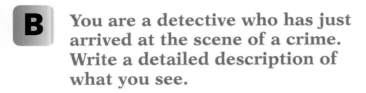

B You are a detective who has just arrived at the scene of a crime. Write a detailed description of what you see.

C Describe the getaway car shown here. Use 40 to 50 words. Underline the adjectives.

Grammar

> A **simile** is a figure of speech comparing two unlike things and is generally introduced by **like** or **as**.
> Example: We had to turn our heads in all directions.
> We had to turn our heads **like a lighthouse beacon**.

A Write the simile.

bee	lion	swan	ox	thieves	bulldog	Punch	fox	dove
eel	Job	deer	Solomon	hatter	wolf	snail		

1. as wise as _____
2. as slow as a _____
3. as slippery as an _____
4. as cunning as a _____
5. as busy as a _____
6. as patient as _____
7. as pleased as _____
8. as swift as a _____

9. as tenacious as a _____
10. as thick as _____
11. as fierce as a _____
12. as gentle as a _____
13. as graceful as a _____
14. as hungry as a _____
15. as mad as a _____
16. as strong as an _____

B These similes show the special qualities of things. Write them.

sturdy	steady	fresh	large	easy	right	tough	cold
	weak	clean	keen	soft			

1. as _____ as a rock
2. as _____ as an oak
3. as _____ as water
4. as _____ as mustard

5. as _____ as paint
6. as _____ as a whistle
7. as _____ as putty
8. as _____ as leather

9. as _____ as A.B.C.
10. as _____ as life
11. as _____ as rain
12. as _____ as ice

C Complete the following sentences by adding striking similes.

1. The rays of light from the camera penetrated the darkness like _____ .
2. The shark's fin cut through the water like _____ .
3. The diver emerged, gasping and snorting like _____ .
4. The sharks glided past like _____ .
5. The submarine rose like _____ .
6. The icy waters pierced my body like _____ .
7. The ship's shadow passed overhead like _____ .
8. Dumas resolutely faced his enemy as though _____ .
9. A dark shadow fell across us and it seemed as if _____ .
10. The men emerged from the water and tired and exhausted, as if _____ .

69

Reading

A   Read the text.

The Battle of Marathon

Marathon, a coastal *plain* about forty kilometres northeast of Athens, was the site of one of the most important battles in the history of Ancient Greece. If the Athenians had lost the battle, Athens would have become part of the Persian Empire, and the history of Europe would have been very different.

In 490 BCE, King Darius of Persia sent an army and a *fleet* of about two hundred ships to conquer Athens. The Persians first destroyed Eretria, a city on the Greek island of Euboea, and then set sail for Marathon. The Athenian general Miltiades positioned his troops on the inland edge of the plain of Marathon, and the Persian army occupied the seaward edge. And they waited. Both sides were waiting for something that would give them an advantage in the battle. The Persians were waiting for a sign that their supporters in Athens had started a *civil war* in the city, while the Athenians were waiting for troops from Sparta.

Both armies waited several days, but neither side received what they were waiting for.

A few days later, the Persian leaders, tired of waiting, and hoping that civil *unrest* had broken out in Athens by this time, loaded part of their army onto ships, and prepared to sail to Athens and attack the city. Seeing their chance for a *victory*, the Athenians charged at the Persian soldiers left behind, and defeated them.

According to legend, General Miltiades sent the messenger Pheidippides from Marathon to Athens with news of the victory. Pheidippides ran the forty kilometres to Athens at top speed, delivered his message, and fell to the ground, dead. Today, the word "marathon" refers to a running race of 42.2 kilometres, *in honour of* the great battle.

When the Persian ships reached Athens a few days later, they found out that not only was there was no civil war in the city, but also that the Athenian army from Marathon had reached Athens before them. As a result, the Persians gave up and returned home.

Activities

A Answer these questions.

1. What is Marathon?
2. Where is Marathon?
3. Why was the Battle of Marathon important?
4. When did the Battle of Marathon take place?
5. Why didn't the Athenian and Persian armies attack each other as soon as they arrived at Marathon?
6. What were the Athenians waiting for?
7. What were the Persians waiting for?
8. Why did the Athenians choose to attack when they did?
9. Explain the connection between the battle of Marathon and a running race.
10. Why did the Persians give up and go home?

B Write the words in *italics* in interesting sentences of your own.
Look up the words in your dictionary if you're unsure of their meaning.

C Wordsearch.
How many musical instruments can you find in the wordsearch?
There are 16.
They can read in any direction.
Challenge a friend!

o	n	a	i	p	l	a	b	b	c	c	d
a	a	b	c	y	p	r	a	t	i	u	g
t	d	c	r	p	i	c	c	o	l	o	d
e	l	e	c	l	s	e	l	d	d	i	f
n	e	o	b	o	e	a	u	a	p	p	e
i	c	d	l	o	r	p	t	p	b	l	t
r	c	t	l	r	o	d	e	f	g	u	f
a	p	l	p	g	r	r	i	u	t	p	t
l	e	r	h	a	g	u	b	o	n	j	o
c	c	p	a	n	a	m	f	d	n	t	p
l	h	l	r	h	n	e	t	u	l	f	g
e	m	s	p	k	e	l	b	a	n	j	o

D These words are often misspelt. Can you write the correct spelling?

1. arguement _____
2. baloon _____
3. beleive _____
4. colledge _____
5. heavan _____
6. heros _____
7. jewellry _____
8. lightening _____
9. marraige _____
10. medecine _____
11. muisence _____
12. ordinery _____
13. pidgeon _____
14. recieve _____
15. resturant _____

Cloze

A   Write the story using the words.

used	hunts	coyote	sacred	call	tried	nothing	once
concentrate	pure	wrapped	stretcher	waiting	symbol
extraordinary	airport	gallery	ambulance

The coyote is a prairie wolf that _____ by night. It is found in Central and North America. The word comes from the Mexican, or Aztec, **coyotl**. (The language of the Aztecs, called Nahuatl, is still spoken today.) It feeds on small creatures and carrion. The coyote was _____ to the American native peoples. They used to _____ him "the trickster".

But for white people, the coyote became a _____ of a menace.

The German artist Joseph Benys, wanted to study the _____ . He wanted to isolate himself with a coyote, to _____ fully on the coyote. He wanted to see nothing else of America – just the coyote, _____ and simple! So, he did an _____ thing. On arriving in Kennedy _____ , New York, Benys was wrapped in felt, laid out on a _____ and whisked in an ambulance to a _____ where a coyote was _____ for him. There was a room in the gallery, divided by a wire grille. He _____ to talk to the coyote. After three days they got _____ to each other's company. Job done, Benys was _____ more _____ in felt, laid on a stretcher and taken to JFK Airport in an _____ . He had seen nothing at all of New York – _____ but the coyote!

Grammar

An **adverb** is a word that modifies any part of speech except a noun or a pronoun. It generally modifies a verb and tells how, when or where the action took place.

Examples:	He sang sweetly.	Modifies the verb sang.
	He ate too quickly.	Modifies the adverb quickly.
	She is very sad.	Modifies the adjective sad.

 A Most adverbs are formed from adjectives by adding **–ly** to the adjective. Examples: wise ... wisely; smart ... smartly.
Complete the following.

Adjective	Adverb	Adjective	Adverb	Adjective	Adverb
1. heavy	_____	6. sweet	_____	11. weary	_____
2. faithful	_____	7. happy	_____	12. quick	_____
3. certain	_____	8. short	_____	13. poor	_____
4. humble	_____	9. skilful	_____	14. hopeful	_____
5. obedient	_____	10. simple	_____	15. high	_____

 B Write the passage and underline the adverbs.

The house at the corner of the street was on fire. I hurried eagerly to the scene. The roof was ablaze. Men rushed frantically about the place with buckets of water. The fire was spreading rapidly, fanned by a still breeze. Blazing beams tumbled to earth as the flames greedily devoured the underlying supports. Showers of sparks burst brilliantly around in all directions, vividly illuminating the spreading shadows of night. In the distance the wailing of the fire brigade's siren could be clearly heard.

 C Write the sentences, replacing the words in italics with adverbs.

1. The doors were closed *in a hurry*.
2. The boy broke the window *by accident*.
3. The cat was lying *in peace* beside the fire.
4. The judge listened *with care* to the jury's verdict.
5. Mina played the piano *with skill* and Amira danced *with grace*.
6. Our aunt comes to visit us *now and again*.
7. I visit my aunt *at regular times*.
8. She spoke *with great anger*.
9. The driver drove the bus *with caution*.
10. *At last* the wedding day arrived.

Writing

> **Quotation marks ("...")** are used when writing the actual words spoken. We call this direct speech.
> When writing sentences, only the words spoken are written inside the quotation marks.
> Example: Helen whispered, **"The money is under the stone."**
> **"The money is under the stone,"** whispered Helen.

A Write these sentences, inserting quotation marks, capital letters, commas and question marks where necessary.

1. John remarked the kestrel is nesting in the ruins of the castle.
2. Tony inquired when will the new cinema open.
3. But that road is closed to traffic interrupted kevin.
4. Dress properly for the interview advised Shin.
5. Why did lantz leave so early asked zindel.
6. She recited the poem beautifully said rani.
7. The singer complained the microphone was not working properly.
8. Maria requested May I borrow your spanish guitar.
9. We have the best football team boasted John.
10. You must answer the question ordered the judge.

> **Remember**: When writing the names of plays, books, newspapers, poems, boats, ships and aeroplanes, use quotation marks '...' and capital letters. Only the important words in the titles are written in capital letters.

B Write the sentences. Insert the quotation marks, capital letters and commas where necessary.
Examples: I saw the pantomime 'Puss in Boots'.
He read 'Huckleberry Finn'.

1. She christened the ship the african queen.
2. I went to see the pantomime snow white and the seven dwarfs.
3. Shakespeare wrote macbeth and hamlet.
4. At our local cinema I saw moby dick, jaws, and mary poppins.
5. Steven spielberg made the film raiders of the lost ark.
6. The twits was written by Roald Dahl.
7. Patrick Pearse wrote the poem the wayfarer.
8. Goldilocks and the ugly duckling are two well-known pantomimes.
9. Jules verne wrote twenty thousand leagues under the sea.
10. John went to see the ballet swan lake.

Language

> **Homonyms** are similar sounding words.
> Examples: **bare** (**bear**), **dear** (**deer**)

A   Write a homonym for each of these words.

1. crews _____
2. hare _____
3. made _____
4. night _____
5. sun _____

6. their _____
7. plane _____
8. waste _____
9. pair _____
10. none _____

11. you _____
12. cellar _____
13. fair _____
14. blue _____
15. here _____

B Write sentences to show the difference in meaning between the homonyms.

1. accept   – except
2. aloud   – allowed
3. board   – bored
4. peace   – piece
5. pray   – prey
6. lead   – led
7. faint   – feint
8. dual   – duel
9. current – currant
10. right   – write

C Write the sentences choosing the correct word.

1. The wind (*blue, blew*) the (*close, clothes*) away.
2. The wedding couple walked down the (*aisle, isle*).
3. The bank reported a healthy (*prophet, profit*).
4. The hunter asked if he (*would, wood*) find a squirrel in the (*wood, would*).
5. The customer paid by (*cheque, check*).
6. The front (*break, brake*) of the bicycle wasn't working.
7. A building (*site, sight*) can be very dangerous.
8. The police arrived at the accident (*seen, scene*).
9. The team celebrated a (*grate, great*) victory.
10. The boat was moored along the (*quay, key*).
11. The golf (*course, coarse*) was extremely difficult.
12. The school (*principal, principle*) addressed the assembly.

Reading

Read the text.

An Intrepid Traveller

It was when she started reading books as a child that Dervla Murphy, Ireland's foremost travel-writer, first developed an interest in and love for travel. Her father was the county librarian in Waterford, and Dervla had access to a wide variety of books which fired her imagination for distant lands and her *determination* to see them for herself. Even as a child she would cycle widely in her native Waterford, and as a young adult she made cycling trips to Europe whenever possible.

Dervla Murphy's first major cycling trip was to India. She made the journey alone, her only companion being "Roz", her old *reliable* bicycle. After the journey, she stayed in India and worked with the Tibetan *refugee* children in Dharmsala. It had been her dream to travel to India and now that this had been realised she set her sights on further horizons.

Three years later, she travelled to Ethiopia and made a long and dangerous trek across the Ethiopian highlands. At the outset, the rough terrain blistered her feet, forcing her to abandon her journey for a week. Her only companion on this adventure was a faithful mule called "Jock". "Jock" bravely *accompanied* her for most of this *gruelling* trip, but due to *malnutrition*, he eventually had to be exchanged for a donkey. Although this was some years before the disastrous famine of 1985, food was very scarce in Ethiopia. Dervla herself lived on the Ethiopian diet of "Injara" and "wat". "Injara" is a *fermented* bread made from "teff", a cereal grain *peculiar* to the Ethiopian highlands. Dervla found it had a bitter taste and it took her a while to get used to it. Generally, the "injara" is served with the "wat" which is a highly *spiced* stew of meat or chicken.

Although she was robbed three times, she generally found the Ethiopians to be warm and hospitable.

In 1979, Dervla set off to Peru with her nine-year-old daughter, Rachel. They spent four months crossing 2,000 kilometres through the Andes, from Cajamarca in the north to the ancient Inca capital of Cuzco in the south. Once more, this was a difficult, *arduous* journey which involved crossing swollen rivers, avoiding dangerous landslides, ascending steep mountain paths and descending into treacherous ravines. The breathtaking scenery of the Andes amply *compensated* them, however, for these discomforts.

Dervla was once asked why she undertook these journeys, which so often involved great *physical* hardship and discomfort. She replied that her idea of hardship and discomfort would be to spend a week in the Hilton Hotel.

Activities

A **Answer these questions.**

1. How did Dervla Murphy first develop an interest in travel?
2. How did she have access to so many books as a child?
3. What four continents has she visited?
4. What did she do in Dharmsala?
5. Why did her mule not complete the journey in Ethiopia?
6. What is the staple diet of Ethiopians?
7. Describe some of the hazards they encountered in the Andes.
8. What does Dervla say about hardship and discomfort?
9. What compensated Dervla and her daughter for their discomfort in the Andes?
10. Write a paragraph about the most interesting journey you have undertaken.

B **Write the words in *italics* in interesting sentences of your own. Look up the words in your dictionary if you're unsure of their meaning.**

C **Common contractions. The apostrophe is placed where the letter or letters have been omitted. He's means He is. Complete the following.**

1. He'd	_____	7. _____	You would	13. Isn't	_____
2. _____	He will	8. You're	_____	14. _____	Had not
3. I've	_____	9. _____	We have	15. Can't	_____
4. I'll	_____	10. They'll	_____	16. _____	Are not
5. _____	You have	11. _____	What is	17. Didn't	_____
6. You'll	_____	12. Was not	_____	18. _____	Will not

D **Wordsearch: Capital Cities. Unscramble the words and find them in the grid.**

1. nolodn _____
2. iroca _____
3. eslssurb _____
4. idbunl _____
5. breraanc _____
6. egahnnepoc _____
7. ituns _____
8. iczruh _____
9. ogsla _____
10. nsateh _____
11. eibrtu _____
12. icnsoia _____
13. ogobat _____
14. antehr _____
15. sloo _____

e	x	p	b	b	o	g	o	t	a	w	p	p
d	n	n	e	g	a	h	n	e	p	o	c	c
l	t	t	k	o	r	i	a	c	x	a	s	h
l	u	t	d	s	x	p	p	n	n	s	s	h
g	r	n	b	i	z	e	g	b	d	n	l	o
a	i	n	s	n	h	r	e	p	h	e	e	l
i	e	i	o	u	h	r	l	l	t	h	s	s
s	b	l	g	t	r	n	o	a	u	t	s	o
o	u	b	a	a	g	n	t	t	r	a	u	k
c	p	u	l	w	d	k	e	s	s	u	r	b
i	p	d	x	o	d	h	s	s	u	r	b	g
n	t	d	n	h	c	i	r	u	z	s	b	d
n	t	e	h	r	a	n	n	k	e	p	o	e

Writing

 A There are 39 deliberate mistakes in this article.
Write out the article correctly
You may need your dictionary.

On 6 March, 1475, won of the world's gratest painters
and sculptors was burn in Italy. his name was Michelangelo.

When Michelangelo was born, his parints were very poor,
though at one time they had been one of the richest familys
in Florence. From his earley days, Michelangelo wanted to
bee an artist. His parents tryd to make him change his
mind, but without sucess. They sent their son to the
famous paintir Ghirlandaio.

Later, Michelangelo enterid the school for
sculptors run bye the powerfull ruler of florence,
Lorenzo the Magnificent. Lorenzo was so
impresed by the young Michelangelos' work
that he took him into his owen household.
Michelangelo remained their untill Lorenzo's
death in 1492.

he was then called to the Vatican and was
asked too work on a tomb that had to be readey
for the Pope when he died.

In 1508, the Pope orderred him to decorate the cieling of the
Sistine Chapel in the Vatican. This work tuck him over four
years, and is to this day one of the finest art tresures in the
world.

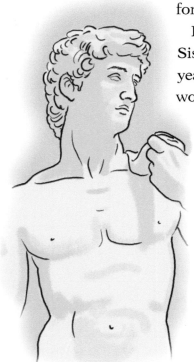

Later, Michelangelo dessigned fortificasions for the town of
Florence, but his heart was in Rome, and he returned their
in 1534.

The Pope apointed him chief sculptor, arcitect and painter
to the Vatican. He bagun to paint his famis fresco, The Last
judgement, on the end wall of the sistine Chapel.

Michelangelo died in 1564 in Rome, but was buryd in
florence.

Grammar

> A **conjunction** is a word used to join words, phrases and sentences together. It can come either at the start of a sentence or between groups of words in the sentence.
>
> | and | but | either (or) | neither (nor) | while |
> |---|---|---|---|---|
> | after | both | for | since | when |
> | although | because | if | unless | whereas |
> | as | before | least | until | yet |

A Write the sentences, using conjunctions from the above list.

1. Anne passed her examination _____ she never seemed to study.
2. The referee looked at his watch _____ blowing his whistle.
3. The tenants hate the landlord _____ he is a cruel master.
4. Jin-Ho will sing _____ you play the piano.
5. Our cat has a long tail _____ a Manx cat has none.
6. He thought the book was stolen _____ he had given it to his friend.
7. My brother is going to buy either a guitar _____ an MP3 player.
8. _____ there is no electricity he will have to use candles.
9. _____ the wall is dry we shall begin painting.
10. The winner was neither proud _____ boastful.

B Underline the conjunctions in these sentences

1. It rained all day and the boys remained indoors.
2. You will fail your test if you don't study.
3. Although I bought a ticket in the raffle I did not win.
4. Either you or I will have to drive the car.
5. I was terrified lest he should jump off the roof.
6. The car was speeding as it passed the school.
7. He will not go to school unless his mother brings him.
8. They started early so that they would finish in time for tea.
9. He speaks as if he knows everything.
10. I felt as though I had been there before.

Writing

A Choose one of the objects below. Write a description of the object using not more than ten single words, for example, small, plastic, and so on. (Do not mention the name of the object itself.) Test your friend to see if he or she can guess the object you have described.

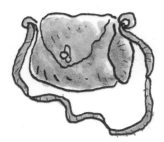  

B You can only use twenty words to describe yourself. You must write sentences, not single words, for both your physical description and personality. Choose your words very carefully.

C

The man in the picture has just won the lottery! Write down ten adjectives you would use to describe how he might be feeling. Example: ecstatic.

D The same man has just realised that he has not got the correct numbers after all. Write down all the adjectives you would use to describe how he must be feeling now.

E You are a reporter who has just arrived at the scene of a bank robbery. What questions will you ask the manager of the bank?

F A genie has granted you five wishes. What will you wish for?

Language

> **Synonyms** are words which are similar in meaning.
> Examples: new (**modern**) laugh (**giggle**)

 A Write two synonyms for each of these words.

1. help	6. difficult	11. friend
2. dangerous	7. sad	12. big
3. brave	8. fear	13. stop
4. still	9. empty	14. tried
5. smell	10. round	15. quick

B Rewrite the sentences, using another word for **nice**.

agreeable	amiable	courteous
delightful	friendly	good
kind	polite	refined
dainty	fine	neat
tidy	trim	luscious
delicious	delicate	soft

1. My father prepared a *nice* meal of steak and onions.
2. The duchess wore a *nice* dress which had *nice* floral patterns.
3. The vines were drooping to the ground with *nice*, ripe grapes.
4. They were *nice* people and they welcomed everyone to the wedding.
5. The *nice* schoolgirl helped the old lady across the road.
6. It was a *nice* evening so the actor went for a walk with the *nice* young lady.
7. The beauty queen had a *nice* soft complexion.
8. The barber gave the young man a *nice* haircut.

C Rewrite the sentences, using another word for **lovely**.
(tasty, interesting, delicious, pretty, daring, thrilling, talented, beautiful).

1. The lovely girl was wearing a *lovely* dress.
2. It was a lovely day so we prepared a *lovely* picnic.
3. The view from the mountain top is *lovely*.
4. The children listened to the *lovely* story.
5. He performs some *lovely* stunts in his latest film.
6. Everybody agrees that she is a *lovely* musician.
7. It is a *lovely* adventure tale set in the Amazon jungle.
8. I ate a *lovely* dinner.

Reading

A Read the text.

The Pharos of Alexandria

The Pharos of Alexandria was one of the seven wonders of the ancient world. Standing over 122 metres high, it was the tallest lighthouse ever constructed, and it guided ships into Alexandria harbour for over 1,500 years.

The city of Alexandria in Egypt was founded by Alexander the Great in 332 BCE and was one of at least 17 cities he named after himself. The other cities are long gone, but the Egyptian Alexandria *flourished*, and is still an important centre for trade today.

After Alexander's death, Ptolemy, the Pharaoh of Egypt, ruled Alexandria. Under Ptolemy the city became *prosperous*, and very soon a lighthouse was required to guide the many trade ships into the busy harbour. The new lighthouse was to be built on the small island of Pharos, which lay just off the coast.

Ptolemy employed a Greek architect, Sostrates of Knidos, to design the building, and construction began in 290 BCE. By the time the lighthouse was complete, 20 years later, Ptolemy had died and his son, Ptolemy II was on the throne.

When the lighthouse was nearing completion, Sostrates asked permission to carve his name into the foundation stone. Ptolemy II refused, saying only his own name would appear on the building. So Sostrates chiselled an *inscription* bearing his own name into the foundation, then covered it with plaster, into which he chiselled an inscription bearing Ptolemy's name. Over the years, the plaster gradually chipped away, removing Ptolemy's name and *revealing* Sostrates'.

The new lighthouse was built on the island of Pharos, and soon the lighthouse became known as "Pharos" too. Being the largest and most famous lighthouse in the ancient world, the word "Pharos" came to be used in connection with lighthouses in general. In fact "Pharos" is the root of the word for "lighthouse" in several languages, including French, Italian and Spanish.

One of the reasons we know so much about the Pharos is that an Arab traveller wrote a detailed description of it nearly 850 years ago. The Pharos was square like a modern tower block, rather than cylindrical (like a modern lighthouse) and was constructed in three stages. At the top, a mirror reflected sunlight during the day, and a bonfire guided ships at night. Sadly, the Pharos was destroyed by an earthquake about 700 years ago.

Activities

A   Answer these questions.

1. Give two reasons why the Pharos was special.
2. Who founded Alexandria?
3. Where was the Pharos located?
4. Why did Ptolemy decide Alexandria needed a lighthouse?
5. Why was the lighthouse called "Pharos"?
6. What favour did Sostrates ask of Ptolemy II?
7. In your own words, describe how Sostrates got what he wanted.
8. In which languages is "Pharos" the root of the word for lighthouse?
9. In your own words, describe the Pharos lighthouse.
10. Why can't we see the Pharos lighthouse at Alexandria today?

B   Write the words in *italics* in interesting sentences of your own.
Look up the words in your dictionary if you're unsure of their meaning.

C   Write one word for each group of words in bold type.
Example: The **girl who played the drums** had long hair. **Drummer**.

1. He made up his mind to go to the concert.
2. The music festival was put off until next week.
3. The pop singer said he was sorry for arriving late.
4. The singer was worn out at the end of the tour.
5. He is recovering his strength at the hospital.
6. The composer wrote his own life story.
7. The festival of light opera is held year after year.
8. The flowers were not real but made of plastic.
9. During the performance smoking was not allowed.
10. Mozart's music is appreciated and played throughout the world.

D   Write a question which you would like to ask each of the following people.

1. An Olympic champion.
2. J.K. Rowling.
3. Neil Armstrong, the first person on the Moon.
4. A newsreader on television.

E   Think of a person in the world you would most like to meet.
Write ten questions you would ask him or her.

Language

Adverbs are words that tell us more about a verb.
Most adverbs are formed by adding **ly** to adjectives.
Example: The bird sang **sweetly**.

A Starting with letters in squares and moving in any direction – up, down, right or left – find the names of nine toys.

```
E  D  D  N  I  R  O  O
T  O  Y  C  A  C  T  T
L  L  A  C  R  S  T  T
I  R  B  A  T  E  A  A
C  K  S  K  I  B  O  O
```

B Brain Teaser.

Linda was in a room where there was just a bath.
The water was running and she couldn't turn the tap off.
There were no doors and no windows.
Linda didn't drown.
Why not?

C Alpha Crossword.
The first letter of each answer is written next to its clue in alphabetical order. Can you find the words, then fit them correctly into the grid? The first letters of all the words have already been filled in.

A. Type of nut (5)
A. Disagree (5)
B. Used for travel on water (4)
D. Precious gem (7)
D. Animal often kept as a pet (3)
D. A pair of singers (3)
E. Not difficult (4)
E. Night (7)
N. Require (4)
O. Tree (3)
O. Single number (3)
P. Fruit (4)
P. A kind of small dog (3)
R. Waterway (5)
S. Large fish (5)
S. Drink slowly (3)
S. Grin (5)
T. Striped animal (5)

© www.puzzlechoice.com

Grammar

A **preposition** is a word placed before a noun or pronoun. It shows the relationship between the noun or pronoun, and some other word in the sentence.
Example: The ball is **under** the table.
The relationship between **ball** and **table** is shown by the word under.

Common Prepositions	about	along	below	by	from	of	until
	above	among	beneath	down	in	to	up
	across	at	beside	during	into	till	upon
	after	before	between	except	near	towards	with
	against	behind	beyond	for	on	under	

A Write a paragraph about a day in your life and include as many prepositions as you can from the list above.

B Write the sentences and underline the prepositions.

1. The gold was in an iron box under the floor.
2. She received a letter from her friend in Paris.
3. The girl stood near the bank of the river.
4. John returned to work after a few days.
5. The call of the bugle awoke me from my sleep.
6. Fools rush in where angels fear to tread.
7. Millions of years ago, dinosaurs roamed the Earth.
8. The raft was swept downriver by the swift-flowing current.
9. The hare ran across the field and disappeared through an opening in the ditch.
10. Aba sat beside her friend during the concert.
11. Before descending, the helicopter hovered above the ship.
12. She left the office at three o'clock sharp and did not return.
13. I hid behind the tree and watched the soldiers marching across the bridge.
14. To whom were you speaking on the telephone?
15. Many domestic animals were drowned during the flood.

C Write an interesting sentence for each for these phrases.

1. accompanied *by*
2. according *to*
3. accused *of*
4. agree *with* (somebody)
5. agree *to* (something)
6. aim *at*
7. angry *with*
8. ashamed *of*
9. blamed *for*
10. capable *of*
11. die *of*
12. differ *from*
13. disappointed *with* (somebody)
14. disappointed *in* (something)
15. disgusted *with*

Writing

 A This Movie Review has been typed by the journalist, but the capitals and full stops are missing. Rewrite the piece correctly.

Latest Movies' Review

i went to the movies last weekend to see the three latest november releases on friday night, i caught "the summer of madness", which was hardly appropriate to this season before christmas however, i did enjoy the weird dialogue between dr. bones and the patient who felt possessed by a witch 'sit down for a spell', the doctor had joked.

early on saturday, i went to see 'throw momma from the train' this was an hilarious send up of hitchcock's 'strangers on a train' at the end i felt like singing the song, 'always look on the bright side of life' i loved the part where danny de vito hit billy crystal's head with a pan and shouted 'you lied'

finally on sunday, i checked out the new adaptation of agatha christie's novel, 'murder on the orient express' this movie was shot during a cold, frosty february and while i thought poirot's accent was more german than belgian, i found the plot absolutely intriguing

B Write a review for your school magazine of your favourite film.

C Write a list of your five favourite books or films.

D Fill out this form that you've just received from the Air Force. (You've just seen an alien spacecraft and alien arrive.)

Alien Sighting Report

Name: _____

Address: _____

Date of birth: _____

Occupation: _____

Where sighting occurred: _____

Time and date: _____

Description of alien: _____

What did it do? _____

What did you do? _____

Have you seen it since? _____

Signed: _____

Language

> **Among** or **Between**?
> (i) **Among** is used when sharing something among more than two people.
> Example: The teacher divided the sweets among the pupils.
> (ii) **Between** is used when sharing something between two persons or things.
> Example: The teacher divided the sweets between Tom and Pat.

A Write the sentences, using **among** or **between**.

1. Uncle Sunil shared the coins _____ Abdul, Bahir and Mahar.
2. Aunt Mary shared the sweets _____ David and Laura.
3. The miser found a gold ring _____ his coins.
4. Deepak left a little space _____ each word and the next.
5. The twins seldom agree _____ themselves.
6. The Irish Sea flows _____ England and Ireland.
7. The two pirates divided the treasure _____ them.
8. The captain divided the sweets _____ the players.
9. The young dancing couple shared the prize _____ them.
10. The coin was wedged _____ the two stones.

> **There** or **Their**?
> (i) **There** – used with verbs: is, are, was, were, has, have.
> Examples: There is a pen on the table.
> There was a pen on the floor.
> (ii) **There** – sometimes means **in** or **to that place**.
> Examples: I went there last week.
> He did not know who was there.
> (iii) **Their** means **belonging to them** – always followed by a noun.
> Examples: I found their dog that was lost.
> Their pet cat ran up the tree.

B Write the sentences, using **there** or **their**.

1. Are _____ any coins in the bag?
2. They put _____ bags over _____ .
3. Will _____ house ever be sold?
4. Some birds obtain _____ food by digging with _____ bills.
5. The whales seized _____ victims in _____ jaws and disappeared.
6. The teacher corrected _____ exercises.
7. We'll meet _____ relations _____ tomorrow.
8. She was _____ when it happened.
9. Scientists come to _____ village to study _____ customs.
10. _____ school team took part in the concert.

Reading

A   Read the story.

Hungry for Gold

Stretching 4,000 kilometres along the coast of South America, the Incan empire of the sixteenth century was larger and better organised than any kingdom in Europe at the time. A road network of some 16,000 kilometres connected all parts, with messages being relayed to and fro by runners stationed every few kilometres along the way. For over one hundred years, a population of some seven million people was ruled by a single family of Incas, who had power of life and death over their *subjects*. Incas worshipped the sun and filled their temples with gold, which they called the "sweat of the sun". The Inca, or king, was believed to be *descended* from the Sun god, and this explains the great power he held over his people.

A Spaniard, named Francisco Pizarro, had heard rumours about treasures of gold held by the Incas and was determined to find it and take it for himself. Hungry for gold, he set off for South America with a small force of 170 men. In 1533, after *enduring* great hardships, the Spaniards reached Peru, where the palace of the Incan King, Atahualpa, was located. The Incas were no match for Pizarro and his men, who easily cut them down with their guns. Atahualpa was captured and thrown into prison. What a *humiliation* this must have been for a king who once said: "In my kingdom no bird flies, no leaf quivers, if I do not will it."

Sensing the Spaniard's lust for gold, Atahualpa decided to bargain for his freedom. He began by offering to cover the floor of his prison cell with the precious metal. So large was this room that Pizarro was totally taken aback by the fabulous *ransom* offer and shook his head in *disbelief*. The desperate Inca misunderstood this *gesture* of Pizarro, taking it to mean refusal; so he now raised his hand above his head and said that, in return for his freedom, he would fill the entire room with gold to that height! A bargain was immediately struck. Messengers were sent to the furthest corners of the empire with instructions for the collection and delivery of the gold. Within a month, the king's subjects had filled the room one quarter full with gold. Atahualpa was true to his word; the Spaniards were not. Fearful of the *consequences* of releasing Atahualpa, the ruthless Pizarro ordered the execution of this last great Sun King of the Incas, on 29 August 1533.

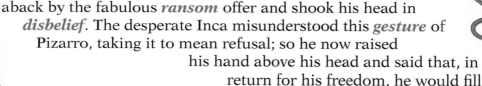

Activities

A Answer these questions.

1. How big was the Incan empire?
2. How did the Incas organise their communications in such a vast empire?
3. Why did Francisco Pizarro set out for South America?
4. How did the Inca or King, come to have such great power over his people?
5. Why do you think Pizarro's journey to Peru was such a difficult one?
6. How did Atahualpa try to bargain for his freedom?
7. Why did Pizarro order the execution of Atahualpa?
8. Pizarro was a ruthless man. What six other words describe the type of person he was?
9. The Incan empire stretched along the length of the Andes mountains in South America. Use an atlas to locate this mountain range.
10. Find out more about the Incas of South America, and write a paragraph about them.

B Write the words in *italics* in interesting sentences of your own.
Look up the words in your dictionary if you're unsure of their meaning.

C Summarise the story in your own words and in about ten sentences.

D There is one error in each sentence. Write the sentence correctly.

1. The cunning fox ran of with a plump chicken.
2. The boy had rang the bell without first looking at the name on the door.
3. She should have went to visit her grandmother yesterday.
4. You and me were very lucky to escape from the fire.
5. Tom or Kathleen must have took the pen.
6. Erina is the smallest of the two girls.
7. The king did not know who had did the evil act.
8. He taught he had made a big mistake.
9. The artist's work is much superior than mine.
10. It was not him who robbed the bank.

E Write the sentences, putting in the correct preposition (**for, on, to, in, with, about, by, to.**)

1. The artist took pride _____ his work.
2. The architect was opposed _____ the building plan.
3. I have the highest regard _____ my uncle.
4. He relied _____ his wife for strength.
5. I was disgusted _____ the man's behaviour.
6. According _____ the doctor the patient was very ill.
7. The team was inspired _____ its captain.
8. The journalist wrote _____ the exciting motor race.

Writing

A There are 35 deliberate mistakes in the following passage. Write the correct words 1–35. You may need your dictionary.

Alexander Graham Bell

Alexander Graham Bell was born in Scotland in 1847. His fater was a techer of deaf-mutes, and Alexander himself showid a great interest in this work.
Alexander's scientific training led him to investigate ways in wich human speech could bee sent by wire.

Tuberculosis was a incurable disease at that time which often prooved fatal. The Bell family, unfortunately, were not to escape. Two of Alexander's brothers died as a result of tuberculosis, and Alexander, also, suffired from the dissease. His father, hoping that a change of climite would help his son, decided in 1870 to move to Canada.

One year later, Alexander's father was invited to go to Boston, U.S.A. to train teachers of the deaf. He felt he was to) old to accept the post, and sent his son along insted. Within two years of taking up the apointment, Alexander Graham Bell became a profesor at Boston Universite.

Here, with the help of a man naimed Thomas Watson, Alexander experimented with electricel transmision of telegraph messiges. Their discoveries led them to exsplore the possibilities of transmiting human speach.

J.P. Reis, a german scientist, had, in 1861, invented a mashine which could transmitt music and noise. He called his invention the tellephone, but it could not transmit the humenvoice.

"Mr. Watson, come here, I want you".

The frist telephone call had been made. Thomas Watson heard the voice over the telephone reciever in another room.

Alexander Graham Bell donatted the money he made from his invention to the deaf, in who he remained interested all his life.

In 1877 he married one of his students, Mabel Hubbard, who was deaf from the age off four.

Alexander Graham Bell died on 2 August, 1922 having conntributed much to the world of science.

Grammar

Common errors to avoid
(i)   **Unique** has no comparative or superlative form.
       Example: This book is unique.
(ii) **Little**, **less** and **least** are used to denote quantity or amount.
       Example: little milk, less sugar, less salt.
(iii) **Few**, **fewer**, **fewest** are used to denote a number of people or
       things.
       Example: few people, fewer corrections, fewer arrivals.
(iv) **Elder**, **eldest** are used for persons of the same family.
       Example: My elder sister is engaged.
(v)   **Older**, **oldest** can be used only for unrelated persons or things.
       Example: This is the oldest car in the race.
       She is the oldest inhabitant in the country.

 A   **Write the sentences, choosing the correct form of the adjective.**

1. The teacher said our school was _____ (*most unique, unique*).
2. Rani has the _____ (*lightest, lighter*) end of the ladder.
3. The four _____ (*best, better*) players are being dropped from the team.
4. Susan is the _____ (*oldest, eldest*) member of the family.
5. Here is the _____ (*more ancient, most ancient*) antique in the museum.
6. Latif held the _____ (*thickest, thicker*) end of the rope.
7. She takes a _____ (*few, little*) lumps of sugar in her coffee.
8. She is the _____ (*biggest, bigger*) of the twins.
9. Which is the _____ , (*taller, tallest*) a giraffe or a camel?
10. The painting is as _____ (*beautiful, more beautiful*) as the photograph.

 B   **Write the words in bold type and write whether the word(s) are a noun, pronoun, adjective, verb, adverb, conjunction or preposition.**

We **were** nearing exhaustion, and cold **was claiming** the outer layers of our bodies.
I reckoned **we** had been down **over** half an hour. Any moment we expected the
constriction of air in our mouthpieces, a **sign** that the air supply was **nearing**
exhaustion. When it came, we would reach behind **our** backs **and** turn on the
emergency supply valve. There was five minutes' supply of air in the emergency ration.
When that was gone, we could abandon our **mouthpieces** and make **mask** dives,
holding **our** breath. That would quicken the pace, **redouble** the drain on our strength,
and **leave** us facing tireless, indestructible creatures which never needed breath.

  The sharks' movements grew agitated. **They** ran around us, working all their **strong
propulsive** fins, **then** turned down and disappeared. We could not believe it. Dumas
and I stared **at** each other. A shadow fell **across** us. **We** looked up and saw the **hull** of
the **Elie Monnier's** launch. Our mates had seen our signals and located our bubbles.
The sharks ran when **they** saw the launch.

  We flopped into the boat, **weak** and shaken. The crew was **as distraught** as we were.
The ship had **lost** sight of **our** bubbles and drifted away. We **could** not believe what
they told us; we had been in the water only twenty minutes.

Writing

A **A Forest Fire**
Imagine you are a member of the fire brigade.
Write a story about a forest fire you once had to tackle.
Use the help words and ideas in the box below.

on duty at the station   emergency call
frantic citizen   forest fire reported
team mobilised
quickly boarded our engines
sirens blaring   bells ringing
through city streets
startled pedestrians and motorists
outskirts of city   dense pall of smoke
pine forest ablaze   fanned by the breeze
spreading rapidly   houses under threat
terrified woodland animals
rabbits scurrying   bounding deer
officer in command   orders
rolled out the hoses
powerful surge of water
attacked the raging inferno
back-up units arrived
five exhausting hours   inhaled smoke
fire under control   finally extinguished
fatigued

B **A Lucky Find**
Use the helpful words and ideas.

storm the previous night
went beachcombing   long sandy beach
screeching gulls   roar of the waves
lonely deserted sandunes
seaweed, driftwood, plastic containers
searched miles of shoreline
about to go home empty-handed
disappointed
just a few metres further
sheltered rocky cove
astonishment and delight
a yacht blown onto rocks
clambered on board   examined
mooring ropes snapped
signs of storm damage
hauled yacht to safety
dashed homewards   notified police
newspaper reporter   photographs
grateful owner   big reward

Phonics

A Descriptive sounds. Write each phrase in an interesting sentence.

| patter | crack | babble | clatter | creak | howling | bang |
| tinkle | clink | dripping | booming | clanking | ring |

1. the _____ of a stream
2. the _____ of a drum
3. the _____ of a gun
4. the _____ of a telephone
5. the _____ of a bell
6. the _____ of chains
7. the _____ of hoofs

8. the _____ of coins
9. the _____ of a whip
10. the _____ of a hinge

11. the _____ of water
12. the _____ of the wind
13. the _____ of feet

B Group terms. Write the group term.

| bunch | suit | army | clutch | team | cluster | choir | forest | band |
| flock | bouquet | suite | fleet | company | troupe |

1. an _____ of soldiers
2. a _____ of actors
3. a _____ of players
4. a _____ of dancers
5. a _____ of angels

6. a _____ of musicians
7. a _____ of stars
8. a _____ of flowers
9. a _____ of eggs
10. a _____ of grapes

11. a _____ of trees
12. a _____ of clothes
13. a _____ of furniture
14. a _____ of ships
15. a _____ of birds

C Diminutive phrases. Write the missing word.

| flake | pat | beam | posy | pinch | ray | blade | morsel | grain | drop |
| sip | wisp | puff | crumb | pinch | grain | breath | sip |

1. a _____ of sugar
2. a _____ of sand
3. a _____ of tea
4. a _____ of salt
5. a _____ of snuff
6. a _____ of water

7. a _____ of butter
8. a _____ of bread
9. a _____ of food
10. a _____ of sunshine
11. a _____ of light
12. a _____ of wind

13. a _____ of air
14. a _____ of snow
15. a _____ of rain
16. a _____ of smoke
17. a _____ of grass
18. a _____ of flowers

Language

A
Commonly misspelt words.
Write the correct spelling. Check your dictionary if unsure.

1. allready, already _____
2. altogether, alltogether _____
3. ammount, amount _____
4. Artic, Arctic _____
5. begger, beggar _____
6. believe, beleive _____
7. beutiful, beautiful _____
8. bicicle, bicycle _____
9. careful, carefull _____
10. cheif, chief _____
11. sentury, century _____
12. dide, died _____
13. disappear, dissapear _____

14. except, egcept _____
15. exsperience, experience _____
16. famaly, family _____
17. forty, farty _____
18. freind, friend _____
19. guard, gaurd _____
20. heroe, hero _____
21. humor, humour _____
22. interested, interrested _____
23. jelous, jealous _____
24. meant, ment _____
25. minute, minite _____
26. prove, proove _____

B
Walked and **went** are too frequently used in writing. In the following sentences choose a suitable verb from the given list to replace the verbs **walked** or **went**. Complete each sentence.

marched	limped	climbed	strode	plodded	prowled	stepped
		crawled	raced	wandered		

1. The defeated team (walked) _____ wearily.
2. The soldiers (walked) _____ quickly.
3. The little baby (went) _____ happily.
4. The brave girl (went) _____ courageously.
5. The tightrope walker (walked) _____ cautiously.
6. The leading athletes (went) _____ .
7. The dark cat (walked) _____ silently.
8. The lost explorer (went) _____ aimlessly.
9. Napoleon (walked) _____ triumphantly.
10. The injured stallion (went) _____ painfully.

C
In the list below, underline the words that give another word when spelled backwards. For example tap = pat; door = rood.

ship	bed	was	room	loot	peels	corn
nib	now	ton	reed	heel	moth	draw
cat	ten	pod	loop	leer	rail	
top	cup	cool	fool	live	gold	

Grammar

A proverb is a wise saying which has been in use for hundreds of years.

 A The proverbs have been mixed up. Write them out correctly.

1. A bad workman is better than none.
2. Necessity can sink a great ship.
3. As you make your bed the mice will play.
4. Make hay while there's a way.
5. Half a loaf make most sound.
6. We never miss the water the sun shines.
7. A small leak blames his tools.
8. Look before spoil the broth.
9. Once bitten think alike.
10. More haste is the mother of invention.
11. When the cat's away so you must lie in it.
12. Where there's a will is the better part of valour.
13. It's a long lane you leap.
14. Too many cooks till the well runs dry.
15. Empty vessels less speed.
16. Discretion that has no turning.
17. Great minds twice shy.

 B Write in your own words what each of these proverbs means.

1. Let sleeping dogs lie.
2. Every cloud has a silver lining.
3. A good beginning is half the battle.
4. A stitch in time saves nine.
5. Every dog has its day.
6. Better late than never.
7. Out of sight out of mind.
8. Birds of a feather flock together.
9. When in Rome, do as the Romans.
10. To kill two birds with the one stone.
11. Practice makes perfect.
12. No news is good news.
13. A rolling stone gathers no moss.
14. Don't count your chickens before they are hatched.
15. The early bird catches the worm.
16. One swallow does not make a summer.

Grammar

> Idioms and colloquialisms are common expressions used frequently in conversation. They have a meaning different from that which appears at first sight.
>
> Examples:
> 1. See eye to eye.   to agree with a person.
> 2. Turn a deaf ear.   not to listen.
> 3. Fight tooth and nail.   to be very determined.
> 4. By the skin of one's teeth   barely, narrowly succeed.

A The sentences below contain colloquialisms. They are in bold type. Re-write these with words which you think have the same meaning.

1. The audience **cheered their heads off** at the end of the performance.
2. It was **raining cats and dogs**.
3. Jane made **a lightning dash** to school.
4. Sunil was **the apple of his mother's eye**.
5. When the teacher talked about the visit the class **were all ears**.
6. Kim and Lin were always **at loggerheads**.
7. Aditi's **heart was in her mouth** when she heard the strange voice.
8. The detective **smelled a rat** when the thief told him where he had got the silver cup from.
9. Mr Smith **kept his wife in the dark** about his plans.
10. After getting all his spellings wrong, Alan had **to face the music**.

B Write the meanings of the following idioms.

1. Hang one's head _____
2. To be tight-lipped _____
3. Turn a blind eye _____
4. Turn the other cheek _____
5. Armed to the teeth _____
6. To hold one's tongue _____
7. To take forty winks _____
8. To be cold-blooded _____
9. Turn up one's nose _____
10. Live from hand to mouth _____